BAKING *for* BEGINNERS

BAKING *for*
BEGINNERS

Easy Recipes and Techniques for Sweet and Savory At-Home Bakes

TIFFANY FRAIOLI &
JAMES O. FRAIOLI
James Beard Award–Winning Author

Skyhorse Publishing

The authors would like to thank Nicole Frail and the marvelous Skyhorse Publishing team for their continuing assistance and support.

Skyhorse Publishing books may be purchased in bulk at special discounts for sales promotion, corporate gifts, fund-raising, or educational purposes. Special editions can also be created to specifications. For details, contact the Special Sales Department, Skyhorse Publishing, 307 West 36th Street, 11th Floor, New York, NY 10018 or info@skyhorsepublishing.com.

Skyhorse® and Skyhorse Publishing® are registered trademarks of Skyhorse Publishing, Inc.®, a Delaware corporation.

Visit our website at www.skyhorsepublishing.com.

10 9 8 7 6 5 4 3 2 1

Library of Congress Cataloging-in-Publication Data is available on file.

Cover design by David Ter-Avanesyan
Cover photo credit by Getty Images

Print ISBN: 978-1-5107-6799-7
Ebook ISBN: 978-1-5107-6800-0

Printed in China

To our children, William and Bianca, for whom we love to bake.

CONTENTS

INTRODUCTION

In Albanian it is *pjekje*; Corsican—*panatteria*; Dutch—*bakken*; French—*caisson*; Hungarian—*sütés*; Italian—*cottura al forno*; Spanish—*horneando*; and Welsh—*polbi*. It doesn't matter where in the world you are or what language you speak—baking speaks the same language to people everywhere. It brings forth pleasant thoughts, feelings, aromas, and memories. Where music is a universal language, so is baking. The smell of fresh baked bread or sweet pastry is very much the same no matter what household or bakery you are in across our globe. Yet—where did this unique form of cooking begin? What was the genesis of this global culinary art form?

A BRIEF HISTORY OF HOME BAKING

Baking began thousands of years ago with a recorded date of home ovens being used by Egyptians around 6500 BC. Ancient hieroglyphs depict images of grains being harvested and milled and then formed into loaves of bread. During this time, the Egyptian people were baking unleavened goods, as the introduction of yeast is not recorded until 2600 BC. Baking was such a revered skill that, during the discovery of ancient tombs, archaeologists found pieces of sour dough bread with the deceased. It is said that bread was put in the deceased's tomb so that the person would not go hungry in their afterlife. The art of creating a stock of sour dough to then start new doughs was probably why Egyptians baked more than fifty different types of bread.

During the Roman Empire, around 300 BC, baking became common in many households. But there was a dividing line between the rich and poor. The rich could afford to bake breads and pastries in ovens with chimneys while the poor could only bake black bread. Grains were milled and baking became such a popular activity that the goddess of bread baking, Fornax, was celebrated each year with a festival. When the Roman Empire spread throughout Asia and Europe, so did the trade of baking.

During the Middle Ages, baking guilds formed. This signified the more sophisticated art of bread baking. Yet, sweeter goods were not produced until the fifteenth to seventeenth centuries. Then, the expensive ingredients of spices and sugar and dried fruits were incorporated into pastries, iced cakes, and pies.

As time and advancements progressed into eighteenth and nineteenth centuries, so flourished the art of baking. Baking became common in households and its simplicity was spurred by the addition of baking powder to give baked products a double boost in the leavening process. Today, not only can one find boxed and prepared products to complete at home, but numerous baked delicacies are pre-made and flash frozen to simply reheat at home. We are fortunate to have a plethora of choices when it comes to baked goods.

With this book, we hope to share with you the option of baking from scratch to give you and your family the joys of baking through the day!

CREATING THE BAKING SPACE AT HOME

Some of my earliest baking memories are when I watched (and later helped) my mother as she masterfully whizzed around the kitchen with a metal bowl cradled in one arm, beating a cake batter with a wooden spoon, while creating one baked good after the other. Our kitchen was not a large one, yet the aromas of fresh baked cookies, breads, and birthday and holiday treats filled the entire house. I often reflect on this memory whenever I glance around my kitchen and think, "I could use more space here . . . or there." It reminds me that genuine home-baked goods can be made in almost any size space. Whether your baking space is small or spacious, here are some tips and advice for creating your own baking "crib."

The overall key to an efficient baking kitchen is organization. By keeping your baking tools and accessories in one area, you won't be dashing throughout the kitchen while prepping your baked goods.

- Make room for your prep. Create **prep stations** for each phase of the recipes. One area can be set aside for mixing with room for the mixer and a place to set measured ingredients and rest scrapers or other tools

used during mixing. If you are starting from scratch, or redesigning your kitchen, including a kitchen island as part of your baker's kitchen is ideal.

- Have another **area set aside for bakers' racks**. Ideally, there should be a spot to rest hot cookie sheets or pie pans when they come out of the oven. The area should be deep—i.e., far away from a child's or pet's curious reach.

- Plenty of **countertop space** will make your work go quicker. Even if you must clear off a space before you begin a recipe, give yourself plenty of room for the prep, production, cleanup, and a final resting spot for your work. If you can install a custom countertop to match your height for kneading bread, that would be great. If you plan on kneading lots of breads, it'll be more efficient to have a counter that is a bit lower for this task. On the other hand, if you don't have other visitors or children in your kitchen when you are kneading dough, you can temporarily use an apple box or step stool to gain height when working with dough. Just be sure to move the box out of the way when your kneading is done. The ideal countertop material for working with bread, rolling doughs, or melted chocolate is marble. When marble is chilled, it helps keep dough from sticking to the surface, especially when you don't want to add extra flour to the dough.

- All tools and accessories should be readily accessible. Use **sliding drawers and cabinet corner lazy susans** for storage of nesting bowls and measuring cups, stackable sheet pans, and other baking tools to make prep for recipes as efficient as possible.

- Before moving into our current home, I checked out the number of **electrical outlets** in the kitchen. I even made sure that we had some outlets on different breakers! There may come a time when you will need to use your mixer, toast some nuts in an air fryer, process ingredients in a food processor, and make hot water in your coffee machine. If you don't have some outlets on different breakers, you may trip a breaker from time to time.

- **Anti-fatigue mats** come in handy. If you have a sturdy (i.e., tile, stone, or concrete) kitchen floor, having an anti-fatigue mat or two really helps relieve stress from working long hours. I keep one in front of my ovens, one in front of my baking workspace, and another in front of my sinks. They not only provide foot, knee, and/or back pain relief, but also are easy to clean after catching dropped ingredients.

ESSENTIAL INGREDIENTS & STOCKING THE PANTRY

Here is a listing of some necessary ingredients in a baker's pantry. It's not all-inclusive, but it covers the important items commonly used in baking:

Baking Powder and Baking Soda. Baking powder is a leavener that makes cakes, bread, and cookies rise. Double-acting baking powder works, as its name implies, twice. It first gives off carbon-dioxide gas when it is mixed with liquid, then it reacts a second time when placed in the oven. Baking powder loses some power after three months. Replace it every three months. Baking soda is another leavener that works when combined with an acidic food product. Carbon dioxide gas is produced from a combination of baking soda and ingredients like buttermilk, cream of tartar, honey, chocolate, and fruit.

Chocolate. It's no wonder chocolate was once used as currency for trade, was a drink of the gods, and a medicine to cure ailments. Cacao beans are harvested, dried, cleaned, roasted, and winnowed (when the bean shells are separated from the "nib" or meat inside). Then they are crushed and heated and cacao butter is extracted. This chocolate liquor is then transformed into many different types of chocolate.

Unsweetened chocolate is often in a small brick of chocolate liquor that has been compressed and solidified. It is usually about 45 percent cocoa butter.

Semisweet chocolate has some sugar added to chocolate liquor that is then solidified.

Chocolate chips are semisweet chocolate bits that can be substituted for semi-sweet chocolate using the same weight.

Store chocolate in a cool place—not the refrigerator. If chocolate is stored in a place that is too warm, some of the oils may rise to the surface or "fat bloom." These grayish white areas are okay, and the chocolate is still usable.

Cocoa powder. Unsweetened cocoa powder undergoes more processing where, during the final extraction, more cocoa butter is removed. The resulting chocolate liquor is then transformed into a fine powder. Dutch process cocoa has been treated with alkali to lessen the bite or bitter taste.

Cinnamon. The bark of a tree, cinnamon is most often available in ground form but is also in stick form. Ground cinnamon is used in cookies, breads, cakes, and pies. Stick cinnamon is used in hot drinks and sugar syrups.

Cornstarch. Cornstarch is derived from corn and is used as a thickening agent. Cornstarch, a.k.a. corn flour, should be stored in a cool, dry place. It is used often in fruit pies, tarts, and sauces. The resulting thickened mixture often has a silky texture and translucent sheen.

Cream. There are several types of cream used in baking and readily available in most stores.

Heavy cream is the richest cream available and is often called whipping cream. This is the ideal cream to use when making your own whipped cream.

Light cream has a lower butterfat content and will not whip but will help thicken sauces.

Half-and-half is half milk and half cream and can be used like light cream. It will not whip.

Sour cream is cream that has been thickened with a lactic acid–producing bacteria. The result is the thick product that will keep in your refrigerator for about ten to fourteen days.

Eggs. Eggs are a common ingredient in baking, adding flavor, richness, texture, and structure. Eggs are available in a variety of sizes and, for consistency, the recipes in my book call for large eggs. Egg cartons are dated with a three-digit code where 001 is January and 365 is the last day in December. Some egg cartons also have a Best By date. The fresher the egg, the better the protein-based, structural quality of the eggs. Do not store eggs in the door of a refrigerator. The storage areas in the door are often a bit warmer than the main shelves of the refrigerator. Ideal egg storage temperature is 40°F.

Extracts. Vanilla is the most used extract in baking. For many bakers, it is difficult to distinguish the difference between pure vanilla and synthetic vanilla in the final products. However, when feasible, use the "pure" extracts, as these have the most genuine flavors. Pure vanilla extract is made from vanilla beans soaked in an alcohol solution. Brands of extracts will slightly vary in their flavor; select the one you like best.

Butter. Nearly all my recipes call for butter. While any brand butter will work for the recipes, butter with a higher fat content (i.e., 82 or 88 percent) will have more flavor, particularly in recipes like buttercream frosting. Should you use salted or unsalted butter? In most recipes, using either is simply a matter of taste. However, you can be safe with using unsalted for nearly all recipes for its sweet and delicate flavor.

Flour. This is the basis for nearly all the recipes in this book and baking in general. Yet there are a variety of flours available and, with the purpose of making "baking your way through the day" simple, here is an explanation of the flours I use in this book.

All-Purpose Flour. All-purpose flour is, as its name suggests, used for most recipes in one's kitchen. It is made from several hard- and soft-wheat flours yielding a protein content between 10 and 12 percent. The protein content of the flours determines the gluten strength. The gluten sheets in dough are

then expanded by the by-products of yeast. All-purpose flour varieties include bleached and unbleached. I prefer to work with the unbleached flours but have not really had a noticeable taste difference when working with bleached.

Bread Flour. Flour with a protein content higher than 12 percent is bread flour. The proteins develop strong gluten in the dough for excellent flavor, chewy texture, and crisp crusts in breads.

Whole Wheat Flour. As its name suggests, whole wheat flour is made from the entire (or whole) wheat berry: the outer bran, the germ, and the heart of the berry (endosperm). In contrast, all-purpose flour is made from just the inside or endosperm. Whole wheat flours are heartier and have a nuttier flavor. They also don't store as well at room temperature for long periods. Normal storage should be in an airtight container in a cool and dark place. But, if you aren't going to use all your whole wheat flour within a month or so, store it in the freezer.

Yeast. Yeast is a living fungus that "comes alive" when combined with flour and liquid. It reacts with the starch in flour by converting it to sugar, followed by carbon dioxide gas and alcohol. In breads, the bubbles get captured by the dough in the gluten, making the bread rise. The ideal temperature for yeast to become active in water is between 105°F and 115°F. If the water temperature reaches 120°F, the yeast will start to die. I like to work with instant or "rapid-rise" yeast, which usually comes in a packet of three with each envelope containing 2¼ teaspoons of yeast.

Honey. Honey varies in flavor and strength depending on where the bees have been when they were gathering their pollen. Whenever I travel, I look for local honey to use in my baking. Generally, the darker the honey, the stronger the flavor. Honey is sweeter than sugar, so it cannot be substituted in equal amounts. If your honey begins to crystallize, remove the jar lid, and heat the jar in the microwave in 10-second bursts until it begins to liquify.

Sugar. Sugar serves as a sweetener and tenderizer, and it turns baked goods into delicious products with a beautiful golden-brown exterior.

Granulated sugar is the most common sugar used in all my recipes.

Confectioners' sugar is powdered granulated sugar used in uncooked frostings and for dusting cakes and cookies.

Brown sugar is granulated sugar flavored with molasses. Dark brown sugar has more molasses and a stronger flavor than light brown sugar. Both these sugars need to be stored in airtight containers to retain their moistness. To measure brown sugar, pack it tightly into the measuring cup.

Maple Syrup. Pure maple syrup is available in various grades. Grade A is made earlier in the season and is lighter in color with a more delicate flavor. Grade B is made later in the season and has a stronger flavor. This is the grade that is used most often in baking. Store maple syrup in the refrigerator.

IMPORTANT EQUIPMENT, TOOLS & ACCESSORIES

Purchase the best equipment you can. After all, you will be using some of it for quite a long time. The most useful tools in the baking kitchen are your hands. They will do most of the kneading, crimping, fluting, pressing, and patting. After that, kitchen tools become an extension of your hands. As your baking experiences progress, you will learn to make do and improvise with kitchen tools. Instead of buying a double boiler, you can use a metal mixing bowl over a pot of simmering water or use an inverted short cocktail glass as a cookie cutter. There's usually always something in the kitchen (or in the house) that will work in a fix.

Cake Rack. Wire racks are made for air to circulate around the baked product so that it cools evenly. It's nice to have at least two—perhaps even one that is round.

Dough Scraper. This handy tool is a must for all bread makers. It looks like a paint scraper but wider. You'll love how it helps lift, turn, and cut dough—so, the bigger the better. It also serves as a handy cutting board scraper.

Grater. You will need a box grater for smaller amounts of food that won't grate properly with the blades of a food processor. The four-sided box grater can be used for fruits, cheeses, and vegetables. A one-sided grater is nice to have, as you can place it over a bowl and grate directly into it.

Kitchen Scissors. This is one tool that I have multiples of in my kitchen. I use it to cut parchment paper, fruits, vegetables, trim pie dough, open packaged food, and more.

Knives. In addition to our standard complement of kitchen knives, bakers should have a chef's knife, paring knife, and serrated bread knife. The chef's knife will take care of chopping nuts and fruits and cutting dough. For smaller jobs like peeling fruits, the paring knife comes in handy. Fresh baked bread is sliced perfectly with a well-made serrated bread knife.

Measuring Cups. You will need two sets: one for dry ingredients and one for liquid ingredients. For a set of dry measuring cups, make sure it includes a ¼ cup, ½ cup, ⅓ cup, and 1 cup. For liquid measuring cups, use the glass Pyrex-type brand that can hold hot ingredients. I think 1-cup and 2-cup sizes are necessary, and a 4-cup is a plus to have.

Measuring Spoons. I recommend having at least two sets in your kitchen. This way you don't have to rinse or wash as you work with a recipe. I also like the sets where each measurement is its own separate spoon. The sets should have ¼, ½, 1 teaspoon, and 1 tablespoon.

Mixing Bowls. A good set or two with various sizes will help you breeze through recipes. Each set should contain small (3–4 cups), medium (8–10 cups), large (about 5 quarts), and one extra-large (7–8 quarts). The bowls can be metal, plastic, ceramic, or glass. A set that includes a spout on one edge is nice to have for pouring batters.

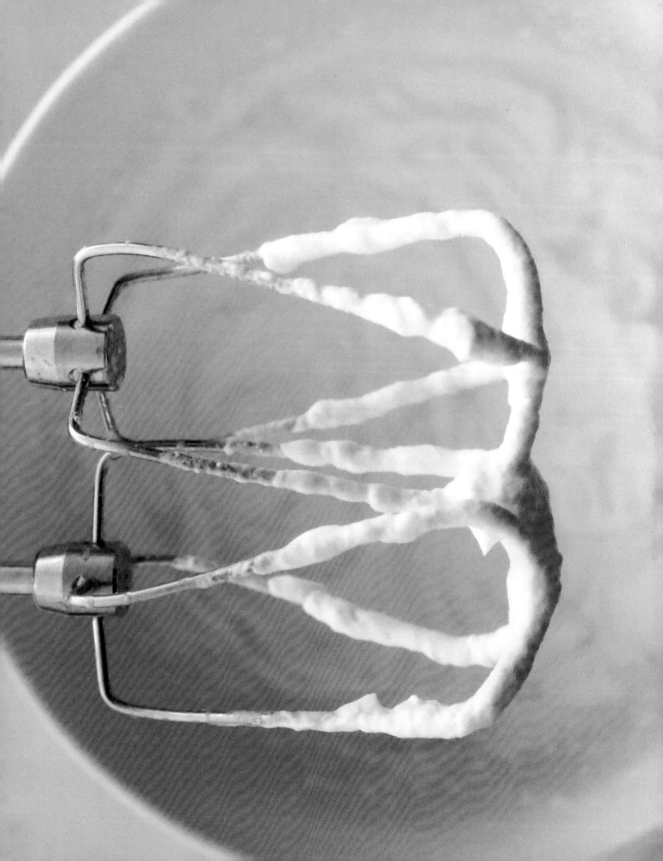

Oven Thermometer. Each one of my ovens has its own thermometer that stands on the oven rack. Some ovens run hot or cold, so it is crucial to know the exact temperature of your oven, especially when you are baking a product for more than 30 minutes.

Pastry Brushes. I have two pastry brushes in my kitchen to use for brushing egg whites on pastries, buttering pans, applying glazes, and even removing crumbs from the tops of topped-off cakes. A good set is between 1 and 3 inches wide.

Rolling Pins. While I have had several rolling pins over the years, I have now narrowed it down to two. One wooden pin, the smaller one, has a roller about 10 inches long. I use this for pie crusts, biscuit, and cookie doughs. The larger one is about 15 inches long and is heavy. I use this rolling pin for working with doughs that should not be overworked: croissants, Danishes, and puff pastry.

Strainer. A small one strains fresh citrus juices, lightly dusts cake pans with flour, and gently sprinkles pastries with confectioners' sugar. A larger strainer sifts flour and other dry ingredients quickly and easily. These simple tools are a snap to clean in no time.

Work Surface. Find a dedicated smooth, flat surface for working with dough, kneading, and chopping ingredients. A marble slab is ideal for doughs that need to stay cool like puff pastry, croissants, and Danishes. Having two options for work surfaces when baking can save time, as you won't need to clean a board before moving along to the next step in a recipe.

BAKING BASICS & PROPER AT-HOME TECHNIQUES

The Recipes. Always read the recipe all the way through before starting. This way, you can assess the equipment and ingredients needed and an approximate time for the prep and the total baking time.

Set Aside Enough Time. After reading through the recipe, you'll be able to figure out how much time will be needed to gather your prep tools, ingredients, and time for not only baking but also cooling. I like to think of baking as a science versus cooking as an art. Science is precise while art styles vary. So, give yourself the appropriate amount of time to be precise in your baking. You'll be glad you did.

Wash. Keep your hands, tools, and equipment clean. Wash hands frequently or, as I prefer, wear food service gloves. Not only do food service gloves keep your hands free of sticky dough, but they also come in handy (no pun intended) if you must quickly answer the phone or open the front door—simply take off the gloves. Clean your baking tools as you go. This helps keep your kitchen organized and lessens the clean-up chore at the end of the recipe.

Gather Ingredients. Before starting a recipe, I gather all ingredients on my baking countertop. If I will be baking first thing in the morning, I often put out the baking ingredients and the corresponding measuring tools and mixing bowls the night before. This way, these few steps are out of the way when I start at the crack-o-dawn!

INGREDIENT TIPS

Don't measure ingredients over the mixing bowl. Place a flexible cutting board on the countertop and then measure your ingredients over that. Since baking is much more of a precise procedure, accidentally adding too much of one ingredient can have a detrimental effect on the final product. Measure ingredients off to one side and then add them to the mixing bowl.

Use butter when it is called for. Don't substitute a spread or reduced-fat product for butter. Use only oils when they are specified, as well.

(Continued on next page)

Don't sift dry ingredients. Most flours have already been sifted, so there is no need for the additional step unless it is stated. Use a wire whisk to mix dry ingredients before slowly incorporating them with wet ingredients.

Temperature of ingredients. In general, it is best to have all ingredients at room temperature prior to starting a recipe. This includes eggs, butter, cream, and milk. When whipping egg whites, make sure the bowl is clean and dry and the egg whites are at room temperature. They will whip up and stiffen better than if they are cold. On the other hand, to whip up heavy cream, it works best when the bowl, beaters, and cream are chilled. My routine is to put the beaters, mixing bowl, and cream in the freezer for several minutes before I begin whipping.

Kitchen Temperature. Doughs with yeast are sensitive to the temperature of the environment in which they are placed to rise. Yeast doughs will rise swiftly in a warm, draft-free area. If the dough is in a cool area, it will take longer . . . sometimes overnight.

Kneading. Here are some basic kneading guidelines: Once the dough has come together firmly in a ball and leaves the sides of the bowl cleanly, turn it out of the bowl onto a clean, lightly floured work surface. Knead for 10 minutes—or whatever time is specified in the recipe. To knead, first stretch the dough away from you. Then gather it back into a ball. Turn the dough about a quarter turn and repeat the process of pulling it away from you then back into a ball. Repeat this until you have turned/kneaded the dough for the indicated amount of time. The average kneading time is about 10 minutes. The texture of the dough will change as it is kneaded to where it will become smooth and elastic. When the kneading is done, place the dough in a clean oiled bowl and lightly oil the top of the dough ball. Cover the bowl with a damp kitchen towel (cotton—not terry cloth).

You can test if the dough has risen properly by lightly pressing a finger into the top of the risen dough (usually 1 to 1½ hours in a 70°F kitchen). It's ready if the dough does not spring back. The rising time is important to keep an eye on. If a dough has not risen enough, the bread will be dense and thick. If the dough has risen too much, there is a risk that the dough will collapse in on itself while it is baking.

Oven Temperature. In yeast doughs, the purpose of a hot oven (400°F) is to kill the yeast activity. So, make sure the oven has been preheated properly to not only stop/kill the yeast fermentation but to also give the bread a crispy crust. For pastries, bake them in the center of a preheated oven. Avoid opening the door before they are done. When done, test them visually or by careful touch and continue baking if necessary.

MORNINGS

I was born to be a natural early-riser—albeit to the benefit of my family, overnight guests, and coworkers. Starting the day with a bundle of energy makes baking morning treats fun. There is also a great satisfaction knowing others in the house will slowly rise to the sweet aromas of freshly baked goodies, such as my Sour Cream Coffee Cake with Cinnamon Topping (page 35) or Banana Chocolate Walnut Muffins (page 29). Or, that coworkers will eagerly taste and appreciate my fresh-baked Strawberry Breakfast Cake (page 39) or White Chocolate Raspberry Scones (page 43). Early-morning bakers like me also have fun baking sourdough breads. Those who enjoy alchemy often fare best with creating successful sour dough starters and are rewarded with a bit more baking freedom during the final baking stage. Unlike other breads, leaving the dough to rise an extra hour or so will not ruin the bread. Whether you make my Original, White, or Rye Sourdough recipe, leaving the dough to rise overnight gives you the leeway to have a hot beverage before shaping the dough at daybreak. A freshly baked, hot slice of sour dough bread gently coated with butter pairs perfectly with a hot cup of coffee. I hope you enjoy baking these morning treats as much as I do.

BAKED AND STUFFED FRENCH TOAST WITH PECAN TOPPING

Here's a perfect dish for your next Sunday brunch or just a fun treat for any morning. Thick slices of sweet egg-soaked bread cooked until golden and crispy around the edges, stuffed with a sweet cream cheese filling, and topped with the sweet goodness of buttery pecans. It's one of our family favorites on the weekend. Although there are many modern twists on classic French toast, like this stuffed French toast recipe, its origin dates all the way back to 300–400 AD to the Roman Empire. In the Roman style of French toast, called Pan Dulcis, they would soak bread in a milk-and-egg mixture, then fry it in oil or butter—like our French toast today.

Serves 6 to 8

CREAM CHEESE FILLING:

2 cups softened cream cheese

1 cup powdered sugar

¼ teaspoon pure vanilla extract

PECAN TOPPING:

3 tablespoons melted butter

1 cup chopped pecans

½ cup lightly packed brown sugar

¼ teaspoon salt

FRENCH TOAST:

4 eggs

½ teaspoon cinnamon

¼ teaspoon ground nutmeg

1. Begin by making the Cream Cheese Filling. Using an electric mixer or standing mixer with paddle attachment, beat the cream cheese until creamy, then add the powdered sugar and vanilla extract. Mix until smooth and creamy.

2. Next, make the Pecan Topping. In a bowl, add the melted butter, then the pecans. Mix until the nuts are coated with the butter, then add the brown sugar and salt until well combined.

3. Preheat the oven to 350°F.

4. Lightly spray a 9 × 13–inch baking dish with cooking spray.

5. To make the French toast, start with a large bowl, and whisk the eggs with the cinnamon, nutmeg, ginger, and vanilla extract. Then add the milk, pumpkin purée, and condensed milk. Continue to whisk until well combined.

6. Next, take a slice of bread and submerge the piece into the pumpkin custard, making sure both sides get soaked with custard. Transfer to the prepared baking dish. Repeat the process until the bottom of the pan is covered with the custard–soaked bread. Then spread the cream cheese filling

¼ teaspoon ground
   ginger

2 teaspoons pure vanilla
   extract

1¼ cups milk

1 (15-ounce) can
   pumpkin purée

1 (14-ounce) can
   sweetened condensed
   milk

1 loaf brioche bread,
   sliced

on top of the custard bread. Soak the remaining bread slices with the custard and place them on top of the cream cheese layer. Finish by sprinkling the pecan mixture over the top.

7. Place in the preheated oven and bake for 40 to 45 minutes. Remove from oven and serve.

BANANA APPLESAUCE MUFFINS

When I'm after a healthy breakfast muffin that's low in sugar, I like to make these Banana Applesauce Muffins for my family. The oil provides healthy fat and antioxidants while the bananas and applesauce provide natural sweetness and the moisture these muffins need. Bananas are also rich in vitamin C and potassium, making these treats my go-to, especially when meal prepping for the week.

Makes 12 muffins

⅓ cup melted coconut or avocado oil

½ cup honey or maple syrup

2 eggs

2 overly ripe mashed bananas

½ cup unsweetened applesauce

¼ cup milk

1 teaspoon baking soda

½ teaspoon salt

½ teaspoon ground cinnamon

1 teaspoon vanilla extract

1¾ cups white whole wheat flour

1. Preheat the oven to 325°F.

2. Prepare a muffin tin lined with paper muffin liners or grease the tin.

3. In a large bowl, whisk together the oil and honey or syrup. Add the eggs and whisk until combined. Add the mashed bananas and applesauce and continue to whisk until combined. Next, add the milk and whisk to combine, then whisk in the baking soda, salt, cinnamon, and vanilla extract. Gently fold in flour with a spatula until combined.

4. Scoop the batter into the muffin tin, filling the cups about ⅔ full. Bake in the preheated oven for 20 to 23 minutes, or until a toothpick inserted into one of the muffins comes out clean. Remove from the oven and let the muffins cool in the tin for several minutes, then transfer the muffins to a wire rack to cool. The muffins will keep at room temperature in a sealed plastic bag for several days, or you can freeze them and thaw as needed.

BANANA CHOCOLATE WALNUT MUFFINS

Banana, chocolate, and walnuts are some of the most delicious ingredients I enjoy in the morning. It seems their flavors always shine through no matter what I'm adding them to. Like my banana, chocolate, and walnut breads, this tasty recipe features the delicious trio in these decadent muffins. One bite and they remind me somewhat of a banana split. I also love the melt-in-your mouth goodness from the melted chocolate and crunchy walnuts. At home, you can whip up these rich and moist muffins in no time.

Makes 24 muffins

2 eggs

¾ cup milk

2 teaspoons vanilla
   extract

1 cup mashed banana

3 cups all-purpose flour

1½ cups sugar

2 teaspoons baking
   powder

1 teaspoon baking soda

½ teaspoon salt

½ cup unsalted butter,
   melted

1 cup diced banana

1 cup chopped walnuts

1 cup granola

1 cup shredded coconut

1 cup chocolate chips

1. Preheat the oven to 350°F.

2. Line 18 large muffin tins with paper liners and set aside.

3. In a mixing bowl, combine the eggs, milk, vanilla, and mashed bananas. Whisk until incorporated and set aside.

4. In a stand mixer with the paddle attachment, add to the mixing bowl the flour, sugar, baking powder, baking soda, and salt. Mix on low until incorporated. Then add the melted butter. Continue to mix on low and add the egg and banana mixture. Scrape the bowl and blend well, but do not overmix. Next, fold into the batter the diced bananas, walnuts, granola, shredded coconut, and chocolate chips. Spoon the batter into the paper liners, filling each one to the top. Place in the oven and bake until the tops are golden brown, and a toothpick comes out clean, about 25 to 30 minutes.

Note: The chocolate will be melted, so when we talk about a clean toothpick, we're referring to the dough mixture, not the melted chocolate. Allow the muffins to cool slightly, remove them from the muffin tin, and serve.

LEMON CRUMB MUFFINS

If you like the taste of lemon meringue pie in muffin form, you must try these breakfast delights. There's nothing like a freshly baked giant muffin made easily from home. Most recipes that yield 12 to 15 muffins will also make 6 jumbo muffins. The trick to getting perfect jumbo-style muffins each and every time is to bake up and not out. That means start the baking at a higher temperature and then, without opening the oven door, lower the temperature for the remainder of the baking. The higher temperature gets that initial rise started and then the lower temperature bakes the muffins more evenly.

Makes 12 muffins or 6 jumbo muffins

TOPPING:

⅔ cup + 2 tablespoons all-purpose flour

3 tablespoons brown sugar, packed

2½ tablespoons granulated sugar

⅛ teaspoon salt

¼ cup melted butter

MUFFINS:

2 cups all-purpose flour

½ teaspoon baking soda

½ teaspoon salt

¼ cup melted butter

½ cup granulated sugar

¼ cup lightly packed brown sugar

2 large eggs

1. Preheat the oven to 425°F.

2. Line a standard 12-count or jumbo 6-count muffin pan with cupcake liners.

3. Prepare the topping in a medium bowl by whisking together the flour, brown sugar, granulated sugar, and salt. Slowly add the melted butter and blend together until small crumbs form. Set aside.

4. To start the muffins, in a medium bowl, add the flour, baking soda, and salt. Whisk together until combined. Set aside.

5. In a large bowl of a standing mixer, beat the butter on high. Add the granulated and brown sugars, and mix until light and fluffy. Add the eggs, yogurt, lemon, and vanilla extracts. Make sure to scrape down the sides of bowl when necessary. Next, add the "dry" ingredients from the medium bowl to the "wet" ingredients in the large bowl. Then add the lemon juice and lemon zest and fold in gently. The batter should be thick.

(Continued on next page)

(Continued on next page)

1 cup plain Greek-style yogurt

1 teaspoon pure lemon extract

1 teaspoon pure vanilla extract

2 tablespoons fresh lemon juice

2 tablespoons fresh lemon zest

6. Divide the batter into the prepared muffin tins, filling about ¾ full. Top with the crumb topping, pressing it into the batter. Do this until each muffin is full.

7. Place the muffins in the preheated oven and bake for 5 minutes. Without opening the oven door, reduce the oven temperature to 350°F and bake for an additional 20 to 25 minutes, or until a toothpick inserted into the muffin comes out clean.

8. Allow to cool slightly before serving.

PUMPKIN PIE BAKED OATMEAL

If you're looking for a delicious breakfast to warm you up on a chilly day, try this baked oatmeal with pumpkin. Not only is it hearty and filling, but it will also keep you fueled throughout the day. The straightforward recipe is effortless to make, and the cooking time is completely hands off. The pumpkin pie baked oatmeal will keep well in the refrigerator for up to four days. For quick breakfasts during the week, I like to make the oatmeal at the start of the week for meal prep. You can eat the oatmeal cold or reheat it in the oven at 350°F for 10 to 15 minutes (until warmed through).

Serves 4

1½ cups quick cooking oats

1 cup unsweetened pumpkin purée

¾ cup milk

¾ cup chopped pecans (reserve ¼ cup for the topping)

¼ cup brown sugar

1 egg

1 teaspoon vanilla extract

1 teaspoon cinnamon

½ teaspoon ground nutmeg

¼ teaspoon ground ginger

1 teaspoon baking powder

1 teaspoon salt

1. Preheat the oven to 350°F.

2. Grease a 9 × 13–inch casserole dish with nonstick cooking spray.

3. In a large bowl, add the oats, pumpkin purée, milk, pecans, brown sugar, egg, vanilla extract, cinnamon, ground nutmeg, ground ginger, baking powder, and salt. Stir well until combined. Then spread the mixture into the prepared casserole dish. Top with the remaining pecans. Place in the preheated oven and bake until the edges begin to turn golden brown, about 30 minutes. Remove from oven and let cool slightly. Serve with milk or heavy cream for extra decadence.

SOUR CREAM COFFEE CAKE WITH CINNAMON TOPPING

Nothing says brunch like homemade coffee cake, and this soft and tender crumb cake using simple pantry ingredients is sure to please. If you aren't familiar, coffee cake is a term given to foods intended to be eaten with coffee or other brunch-type foods. For me, the cinnamon topping is where this cake really shines. It's layered both inside the cake *and* on top, adding that cinnamon sweetness throughout with the perfect crunch on top.

Serves 9

CINNAMON STREUSEL:

1¾ cups all-purpose flour

1 cup lightly packed brown sugar

1 teaspoon cinnamon

½ teaspoon salt

¾ cup cold butter, cubed

COFFEE CAKE:

2 cups all-purpose flour

1¼ teaspoons baking powder

½ teaspoon baking soda

½ teaspoon salt

½ cup softened butter

½ cup granulated sugar

2 large eggs

2 teaspoons pure vanilla extract

1 cup sour cream

1. Preheat the oven to 350°F.

2. Lightly spray a 9 × 9–inch casserole or baking dish.

3. Begin by making the cinnamon streusel. In a medium bowl, add the flour, brown sugar, cinnamon, salt, and butter. Use a pastry cutter to blend (the butter should be the size of peas when you are done). Set aside.

4. In a medium bowl, start the coffee cake, by adding the flour, baking powder, baking soda, and salt. Whisk until well combined.

5. In a large bowl, beat together the butter and sugar until light and fluffy. Add the eggs, vanilla, and sour cream. Note: Use a hand mixer if you have one. Next, add the "dry" ingredients from the medium bowl in batches into the "wet" ingredients in the large bowl. Mix well until incorporated.

6. Next, add half of the batter to the prepared baking dish and top with half of the streusel. Then cover the streusel with the remaining batter and top again with the remaining streusel, ensuring it is spread evenly.

7. Bake in the preheated oven for approximately 50 minutes, or until a toothpick comes out clean when inserted.

8. Let cool slightly and serve.

STRAWBERRY TOASTER PASTRIES

If you like Pop-Tarts, you will love my from-scratch toaster pastries. These homemade treats mean none of those unrecognizable ingredients like xanthan gum, soy lecithin, and red 40. Instead, you will enjoy all that strawberry goodness with plenty of frosting, just like the originals. When making at home, you might find crafting these pastries isn't the easiest, but this recipe should not intimidate you. Just take your time, read the instructions before beginning, and be patient. Believe me, the result will be well worth your time and effort.

Makes 8 toaster pastries

DOUGH:

4 cups all-purpose flour

1 tablespoon white sugar

1 teaspoon fine sea salt

1 cup cold butter, cubed

¼ cup ice water (more if needed)

Egg wash: 1 large egg, beaten with 1 tablespoon of heavy cream (or milk)

FILLING:

1 cup fresh market strawberry jam

2 tablespoons cornstarch

GLAZE:

2 cups powdered sugar

¼ cup buttermilk

Confetti sprinkles, as needed (optional)

1. To start the dough, use a food processor to combine the flour, sugar, and salt. Add the cubed butter and pulse until combined. With the motor running, slowly stream in the ice water, a little at a time, until the dough begins to form a ball. Note: The dough can also be made by hand by cutting the butter into the flour with a pastry blender then stirring in the ice water.

2. Divide the dough in half, shaping each piece into a flattened disc. Wrap each disc securely in plastic wrap. Refrigerate the dough for 15 minutes.

3. Next, lightly flour a flat, even work surface and, using a rolling pin, roll out each piece of dough into a 16 × 20–inch rectangle roughly ⅛ inch thick. Use a ruler to measure out 8 (4 × 5–inch) rectangles.

4. To make the filling, combine the strawberry jam and cornstarch until mixed well and divide evenly between 8 rectangles.

5. Brush the egg wash around the edges of the dough and cover with the other 8 pastry rectangles. Crimp the edges with a fork to make sure they are sealed, or the filling will ooze out. Chill in the refrigerator for at least 30 minutes.

6. Preheat the oven to 350°F.

7. Brush the chilled pastries with the remaining egg wash. Bake for 20 minutes, or until golden brown. Allow to cool while making the glaze.

8. In a medium bowl, whisk together the powdered sugar and buttermilk until smooth. Drizzle or spoon the glaze on top of the completely cooled toaster pastries then top with sprinkles, if desired.

STRAWBERRY BREAKFAST CAKE

Breakfast cakes, like this one, have grown in popularity, and for good reason. They're a wonderful way to showcase fresh, seasonal fruits in a simple and delicious all-purpose cake. What I enjoy about this cake is it's not overly sweet, especially for breakfast, and I love the light, cream batter. When selecting strawberries for this dish, I like firm, ripe berries from local farmers. They're usually fresher and better flavored. Remember, with most fruit-centric recipes, the better the fruit, the better the result.

Makes 1 (9-inch) cake

2¼ cups all-purpose flour, divided

½ teaspoon salt

2½ teaspoons baking powder

¼ teaspoon baking soda

½ cup granulated sugar

1 cup diced strawberries

½ cup melted butter

1 cup sour cream

2 teaspoons pure vanilla extract

2 large eggs

1 cup plain Greek-style yogurt

Powdered sugar, for serving

1. Preheat the oven to 350°F.

2. Lightly grease and flour a 9-inch springform pan.

3. In a large mixing bowl, whisk together 2 cups of the flour, salt, baking powder, baking soda, and granulated sugar. Set aside.

4. In a small bowl, combine 1 cup diced strawberries with the remaining ¼ cup of flour. Toss the strawberries in the flour.

5. In a separate small mixing bowl, combine the melted butter, sour cream, vanilla, and the eggs. Fold together with a spatula until well combined. Add the Greek-style yogurt mixture to the flour and sugar. Mix all the ingredients together. Note: The batter will be thick. Add the floured strawberries and any extra flour and combine. Place the mixture in the prepared pan and bake for 1 hour, or until a toothpick inserted in the middle comes out clean. The top should be golden brown.

6. Remove from the oven and let cool, then sprinkle with powdered sugar, if desired. This cake is best served fresh and warm.

TOASTED VANILLA GRANOLA

The beauty of this healthy, delicious granola is you can use almost anything you have on hand to make it—pretty much any nut or seed will do. My family's favorite is a combination of chopped hazelnuts, walnuts, almonds, and pumpkin seeds. It's hard to resist this fresh homemade granola (while making your entire house smell heavenly while it bakes). The granola is perfect on its own, or added to yogurt, fresh fruit, ice cream, or in other baking recipes.

Makes about 4 cups

3 cups rolled oats

2 cups chopped nuts and/or seeds of your liking

1 teaspoon cinnamon

¼ cup coconut oil

¼ cup agave nectar

1 tablespoon pure vanilla extract

1. Preheat the oven to 300°F.

2. Line a baking sheet with a nonstick baking mat. If you don't have a mat, simply use parchment paper.

3. In a large mixing bowl, add the oats, nuts, seeds, and cinnamon. Stir to combine.

4. In a small, microwave-safe bowl, add the coconut oil and microwave until melted, about 1 minute. Add the agave nectar, whisk to combine, and microwave again until warm, about another minute. Add the vanilla extract and whisk to combine.

5. Pour the "wet" ingredients over the "dry" ingredients in the bowl, and stir until all the oats, nuts, and seeds are completely covered. Then spread the mixture onto the prepared baking sheet. Spread out in one thin and even layer. Place in the oven and bake until the edges of the granola are just beginning to color, about 25 to 30 minutes.

6. Allow the granola to cool entirely before breaking it up into smaller pieces. Note: The granola will get crunchy as it cools. Store in an airtight container until ready to serve or enjoy immediately.

WHITE CHOCOLATE RASPBERRY SCONES

If you're looking for a soft, decadent treat loaded with sweet and tart flavors, this breakfast or brunch accompaniment is a must. Fresh raspberries bursting with flavor along with creamy white chocolate combine for the perfect pairing. Be sure to use fresh raspberries, as frozen raspberries tend to turn mushy—even when defrosted—which can easily turn your batter watery. If you've never attempted making scones before, you're in for a pleasant surprise, as they're simple to make so long as you don't overwork the dough. To help dice the cold butter, I like to use a pastry cutter or box grater. The key is getting the cold butter into little pieces, like the chocolate.

Makes 8 scones

2 cups all-purpose flour

1 teaspoon baking powder

¼ teaspoon baking soda

½ teaspoon salt

⅓ cup + 1 tablespoon white sugar

½ cup cold unsalted butter, diced

½ cup sour cream

1 egg

1 cup fresh raspberries

½ cup white chocolate, broken into little pieces

1. Preheat the oven to 400°F.

2. In a large mixing bowl, add the flour, baking powder, baking soda, salt, and sugar. Stir to combine the dry ingredients. Cut in the diced butter and continue until the mixture resembles a coarse meal. Set aside.

3. In a small bowl, whisk together the sour cream and egg. Then pour into the dry ingredients and stir until combined. At this stage, the dough should be coarse and dry.

4. Flour your hands and form the dough into a ball, being careful not to overwork the dough. We're after fluffy (not dense) scones.

5. Place the dough ball on a flour-dusted countertop and lightly knead to form a circle about 7 inches wide. Then carefully add the fresh raspberries and chocolate evenly over the top of the dough. Gently knead the dough again so the raspberries and chocolate get blended throughout. During this process, the berries will begin to break down a bit, creating colorful swirls. Now, lightly knead again to form a circle about 7 inches wide. Using a pizza cutter, slice the dough into 8 wedges.

6. Transfer the scones to a cookie sheet and bake until light brown, about 16 or 17 minutes. Remove from the oven and allow to cool slightly before serving.

APPLE, ONION, AND BACON SCONES

I love these homemade apple, onion, and bacon scones. They're savory, crumbly, and incredibly delicious. I like to serve them for breakfast or as a side dish at brunch. If you've never made a scone, they're like baking biscuits but are a bit heartier and heavier. I also find them to be one of the easiest pastries to make. I prefer Gala apples for this recipe. They have a sweet flavor with hints of vanilla and a floral aroma.

Makes 8 scones

3 cups all-purpose flour

1 tablespoon baking powder

2 tablespoons granulated sugar

1 teaspoon salt

½ cup cold unsalted butter

1 cup sautéed sweet onions

3 strips cooked bacon, roughly chopped

1 cup peeled, diced apples

1 cup buttermilk

1 egg

1 tablespoon cold water

1. Preheat the oven to 400°F.

2. Line a baking sheet with parchment paper and set aside.

3. In a mixing bowl, add the flour, baking powder, sugar, and salt. Whisk together until combined. Then make a well in the center of the dry ingredients. Shred the butter through a large-holed box grater held over the dry ingredients. Gently toss the butter shreds with the dry mixture, to coat. Next, fold in the sautéed onion, bacon, and apple pieces. Then pour in the buttermilk and stir gently until dough just comes together. The dough will be sticky. Scrape the dough onto the prepared baking sheet. Moisten your hands with a touch of cold water before lightly patting the dough into a level, 8-inch-diameter circle. Dip a knife into the flour and carefully score the dough into 8 wedges. To score, cut most of the way through the dough, but not entirely through to the bottom. Do not separate the wedges.

4. Create an egg wash by beating the egg with the cold water. Then brush the egg wash over top of the dough.

5. Bake the scones in the preheated oven for 18 to 20 minutes, or until golden brown. Remove from the oven and allow to cool for several minutes on the baking sheet before transferring to a wire rack to cool completely. Before serving, cut the scones into wedges following the scored marks made prior to baking. The scones are best served warm.

CHEDDAR AND CHIVE SCONES

Here's another savory scone I encourage you to make at home. They're moist and flavorful with crisp, crumbly edges, perfect for your next breakfast, brunch, or wherever muffins and coffee are served. Enjoy these cheesy herbed scones fresh from the oven with a spread of butter or cool them down to serve later.

Makes 8 scones

3 cups flour

1 tablespoon baking powder

1 tablespoon sugar

1 teaspoon salt

1½ cups sharp cheddar cheese, grated

½ cup fresh chives, finely chopped

2 cups heavy cream + more for brushing

1. Preheat the oven to 400°F.

2. Line a baking sheet with parchment paper and set aside.

3. In a mixing bowl, add the flour, baking powder, sugar, and salt. Mix well to combine, then add the cheese and chives. Stir the mixture thoroughly to combine. Then slowly pour in the cream and mix with a fork until a sticky dough clump forms. Knead the dough about 10 times and then press the ball onto a floured surface, pushing down until a circle about 8 inches in diameter is formed. The dough should be about ¾ inch thick.

4. Cut the dough into 8 triangles. Place the triangles onto the prepared baking sheet about 1 inch apart. Brush top with some additional cream and bake in the preheated oven for about 20 minutes, or until the scones are golden brown.

ENGLISH MUFFINS

Here's my recipe for homemade English Muffins. They're soft, chewy, and simply delicious. The recipe is very easy, although I like to bake these muffins on the weekend and serve them to my family with butter and jam or as part of an eggs Benedict breakfast. Best part of all, they're much tastier and healthier compared to those storebought muffins. Try them and I bet you'll be making them repeatedly.

Makes 16 muffins

2 cups whole milk

3 tablespoons honey

1 packet (2¼ teaspoons) active dry yeast

1 large egg

4 tablespoons unsalted butter, melted

5 cups bread flour

1½ teaspoons salt

Cornmeal, as needed, for dusting

1. In a small saucepan, heat the milk and honey over low heat until it reaches 105°F to 115°F. Note: Use a candy or digital thermometer. Remove from the heat, stir in the yeast, and set aside for 5 minutes, then whisk in the egg and melted butter.

2. Add the flour and salt to the bowl of a stand mixer. Fit the mixer with the dough hook attachment. With the mixer on low speed, gradually pour the milk mixture into the flour.

3. Continue to beat on low until the flour is incorporated, stopping to scrape down the sides and bottom of the bowl as needed. Increase the speed to medium and mix for about 4 minutes, or until the dough clears the sides of the bowl and is smooth and elastic. The dough should feel slightly tacky when gently pressed with your fingertip.

4. Scrape the dough out into a lightly oiled bowl. Brush a little oil over the top of the dough. Cover and set in a warm place to rise for 1 hour or until the dough doubles in size.

5. Gently punch the dough down and turn it out onto a lightly floured surface. Gently knead the dough together into a ball and divide it in half. Divide each half into 8 equal-sized pieces. You should have 16 dough balls. Note: If you want smaller muffins, divide each half into 11 pieces to equal 22 dough balls. Roll each piece into a ball and flatten the

(Continued on next page)

ball into a disc. Note: If the dough is too sticky, lightly oil your hands to make it easier to handle the dough.

6. Place the discs on a baking sheet lined with parchment paper that has been dusted with cornmeal. Sprinkle more cornmeal over the tops. Cover with a lint-free towel and set in a draft-free place for 1 hour, or until doubled in size.

7. Preheat the oven to 325°F.

8. Heat a griddle over medium-low heat. Gently lift each disc with a plastic spatula and place it on the griddle. Note: Handle the dough with care so you don't deflate it. Cook them for about 2 minutes on each side, until lightly browned on both sides. Work in batches.

9. Place the muffins back on the cookie sheet and bake them for 10 to 15 minutes. The internal temperature should be about 200°F on an instant-read thermometer.

10. Transfer the muffins to a cooling rack and let them cool completely.

11. Split the English muffins with a fork and toast them in a toaster until the edges are lightly browned.

HASHBROWN-CRUSTED QUICHE

This Hashbrown-Crusted Quiche is a fun twist on the traditional quiche. The hashbrowns offer a crisp and crunchy crust compared to dough. It's a great texture to add to this light and fluffy quiche that's filled with cheese and sausage, making it the perfect meal for breakfast or brunch. For the shredded potatoes, you can make your own hashbrowns from scratch or purchase storebought. Personally, I find the freezer hash browns at the supermarket work great for this recipe.

Makes 6 to 8 slices

3 cups shredded potatoes

¼ cup melted butter

Salt, as needed, to taste

Fresh cracked black pepper, as needed, to taste

1 cup mild Italian pork sausage

6 large eggs

¼ cup heavy cream

1 cup shredded cheddar cheese

1 cup shredded Monterey jack cheese

2 scallions, finely chopped

1. Preheat oven to 375°F.

2. Coat a 9-inch pie plate with nonstick cooking spray.

3. In a large bowl, gently toss the shredded potatoes with the melted butter to coat. Then season with salt and pepper. Press the hashbrowns into the bottom and up the sides of the plate to form a crust. Bake in the preheated oven for about 25 to 30 minutes, or until golden brown.

4. Meanwhile, sauté the ground sausage in a skillet over medium-high heat, breaking it up with a wooden spoon, until no longer pink, about 5 minutes. Set aside to cool.

5. In the large bowl you used for the hashbrowns, add the eggs, cream, cheeses, and scallions. Whisk to combine and season with salt and pepper. Add the cooked sausage crumbles. Mix to combine.

6. Pour the mixture on top of the hashbrown crust. Bake for about 30 minutes or until set. Cut the quiche into wedges and serve immediately.

SOURDOUGH STARTER

There is one universally accepted rule when it comes to baking breads: weigh rather than measure. To achieve the absolute best bread-baking results, invest in a high-quality kitchen scale that will assure pin-point accuracy. Remember, bread making is a science, and this top-notch sourdough starter—a concoction of whole wheat flour and water that hosts a stable blend of beneficial bacteria and wild yeasts—takes weight into account. The combination is constantly maintained with regular refreshments and is used to leaven and flavor new bread dough. If you missed the craze of making your own sourdough starter during the pandemic, feel free to dive in with this winning recipe.

DAY 1:

500 grams (1.1 pounds) whole wheat flour
500 grams (2.2 cups) warm water

In a large bowl (or 6-quart round plastic tub with lid), add the flour and water and mix by hand until incorporated. Leave the "mix" uncovered for up to two hours, then cover with plastic wrap and leave in a warm place overnight.

DAY 2:

Throw away approximately ¾ of the slurry mix and leave the remainder in the bowl. Add another 500 grams of whole wheat flour and 500 grams of warm water and mix again until incorporated. Leave uncovered for up to 2 hours then cover and leave in a warm place overnight.

DAY 3:

The slurry mix should now be about double the volume. Again, throw away ¾ of the mixture and add 500 grams whole wheat flour and 500 grams warm water and mix until combined. Leave uncovered for up to two hours then cover and leave in a warm place overnight.

DAY 4:

Throw away all but 200 grams (about 7 ounces). Note: Weigh the bowl/tub before starting so you know how many grams you need to reserve of the starter. Be accurate with this measurement; this will ensure your bread's success. Add another 500 grams of whole wheat flour and 500 grams of warm water and combine until mixed well with starter. Cover and let rest in warm place.

The starter is ready to use. To prepare for baking, throw away 150 grams (about 5.3 ounces) of starter. Then add 400 grams (about 14 ounces) of white flour and 100 grams (about 3.5 ounces) of whole wheat flour and 400 grams (about 14 ounces) of warm water. Mix. Cover and let it rest in a warm place. Note: Ideally, do this in the morning so you can make your bread in the afternoon and leave to rest overnight.

ORIGINAL SOURDOUGH BREAD

Homemade artisan sourdough bread is delightfully easy to make with just a Dutch oven as the perfect baking vessel. If you have a wood-fired oven, your sourdough bread will take on a delicious, smoky flavor. This recipe will guide you step-by-step through the easy-to-prepare sourdough bread process. Remember that the starter you use must be strong and active to impart a pungently fragrant flavor to the bread.

Makes 2 loaves

750 grams white flour

50 grams whole wheat flour

660 grams warm water

2 grams instant yeast

20 grams fine sea salt

360 grams Sourdough Starter, page 54

1. Mix the white and whole wheat flours together with the warm water and let sit covered for 30 minutes.

2. Add the yeast and salt into the dough then add the starter and mix until combined. Fold the dough 2 or 3 times (every 30 minutes) until fully incorporated and let rest about 5 hours, or until the dough doubles from its original size.

3. Divide the dough into two equal rounds. Next, shape the dough into loaves, using either dusting baskets or two medium-sized bowls. Place the dough back in the baskets or bowls, cover with plastic wrap, and refrigerate overnight.

4. Place a Dutch oven, with the lid on, into the oven.

5. Preheat the oven to 500°F with the Dutch oven inside, for 30 minutes.

6. Being extremely careful, remove the Dutch oven from the oven and remove the lid. Drop the dough into the Dutch oven and replace the lid. Transfer the Dutch oven back into the oven for 30 minutes. Remove the lid and bake another 20 to 30 minutes, or until the sourdough's crust is a dark golden brown. Carefully remove the sourdough from the Dutch oven and let cool on a wire rack for at least 10 minutes before cutting into the loaf.

7. Repeat with the remaining dough.

WHOLE WHEAT SOURDOUGH BREAD

Today's health consciousness is slowly being built into our DNA—like it or not. Before selecting a food to dine on, many people stop to consider if it is a "healthier choice." Since I believe this is a good thing, I included a healthy Whole Wheat Sourdough Bread recipe in this section. If you like darker breads, whole wheat is a smart choice. The fact is whole wheat breads tend to be more flavorful, too. The tanginess of the sourdough combined with the nuttiness of the whole wheat flour yields a wholesome taste. Whether you use it for sandwiches, a side accompaniment with soups or stews, toast and butter, or even crunchy croutons, this recipe will provide plenty of crunch and culinary excitement for your taste buds.

Makes 2 loaves

90 grams white flour

710 grams whole wheat flour

660 grams warm water

2 grams instant yeast

20 grams fine sea salt

360 grams Sourdough Starter, page 54

1. Mix the white and whole wheat flours together with the warm water and let sit covered for 30 minutes.

2. Add the yeast and salt into the dough then add the starter and mix until combined. Fold the dough 2 or 3 times (every 30 minutes) until fully incorporated and let rest about 5 hours, or until the dough doubles from its original size.

3. Divide the dough into two equal rounds. Next, shape the dough into loaves, using either dusting baskets or two medium-sized bowls. Place the dough back in the baskets or bowls, cover with plastic wrap, and refrigerate overnight.

4. Place a Dutch oven, with the lid on, into the oven.

5. Preheat the oven to 500°F with the Dutch oven inside, for 30 minutes.

6. Being extremely careful, remove the Dutch oven from the oven and remove the lid. Drop the dough into the Dutch oven and replace the lid. Transfer the Dutch oven back into the oven for 30 minutes. Remove the lid and bake another 20 to 30 minutes, or until the sourdough's crust is a dark golden brown. Carefully remove the sourdough from the Dutch oven and let cool on a wire rack for at least 10 minutes before cutting into the loaf.

7. Repeat with the remaining dough.

RYE SOURDOUGH BREAD

Sourdough rye is best described as dark, dense, and aromatically pungent. It is often served thinly sliced with pastrami or smoked salmon. As with all sourdoughs, rye sourdough is delicious toasted with a light topping of butter or aged cheddar cheese. Be sure to let your dough rise in a room that is warm, and keep the covering of the dough moist. This recipe is a step-by-step guide to making this very delicious bread at home. Before you know it, you will be a pro at making Rye Sourdough Bread with its pleasingly unique flavor.

Makes 2 loaves

540 grams white flour

180 grams rye flour

80 grams whole wheat flour

660 grams warm water

2 grams instant yeast

20 grams fine sea salt

360 grams Sourdough Starter, page 54

1. Mix the white, rye, and whole wheat flours together with the warm water and let sit covered for 30 minutes.

2. Add the yeast and salt into the dough then add the starter and mix until combined. Fold the dough 2 or 3 times (every 30 minutes) to fully incorporated and let rest about 5 hours, or until the dough doubles from its original size.

3. Divide the dough into two equal rounds. Next, shape the dough into loaves, using either dusting baskets or two medium-sized bowls. Place the dough back in the baskets or bowls, cover with plastic wrap, and refrigerate overnight.

4. Place a Dutch oven, with the lid on, into the oven.

5. Preheat the oven to 500°F with the Dutch oven inside, for 30 minutes.

6. Being extremely careful, remove the Dutch oven from the oven and remove the lid. Drop the dough into the Dutch oven and replace the lid. Transfer the Dutch oven back into the oven for 30 minutes. Remove the lid and bake another 20 to 30 minutes, or until the sourdough's crust is a dark golden brown. Carefully remove the sourdough from the Dutch oven and let cool on a wire rack for at least 10 minutes before cutting into the loaf.

7. Repeat with the remaining dough.

AFTERNOONS

One of my goals with this book is to encourage aspiring bakers—young and old—to gain confidence in mastering their baking skills. Baking from scratch, as it should be, is an easy way to explore all the wonderful grains of our Earth. Some of the best baking recipes are those that can be prepared in the afternoon. What better way to welcome children home from school than with a warm, just-out-of-the-oven slice of homemade Walnut Banana Bread (page 79), a piece of freshly frosted Pumpkin Square with Cream Cheese Frosting (page 75), or a hot slice of Dark Chocolate Zucchini Bread (page 67). The late-day hours are also ideal for preparing some savory breads to serve with dinner. In this section, you'll read how deliciously easy it is to make classic Rosemary Focaccia (page 91) and Tomato Focaccia (page 95). These traditional Italian breads can be served as an antipasto with a dish of virgin olive oil/vinegar and a lovely tray of salami and soppressata. When the grill is in use and you've got a juicy T-bone or barbecued chicken for dinner, a side serving of Jalapeño Bacon Bread (page 90) will certainly hit the spot.

BANANA BREAD

When it comes to bananas, this is one of my favorite recipes. Not only is it easy to follow, but the result showcases loads of bananas, toasted walnuts, and hidden gems of chocolate nestled throughout the deliciously moist bread. This recipe is also a great way to use those overripe bananas that may be sitting on your counter.

Makes 1 loaf

3–4 extremely ripe bananas

½ cup melted butter

2 large eggs

¼ cup granulated sugar

1 teaspoon pure vanilla extract

½ teaspoon salt

2 cups flour

1 teaspoon baking soda

1 teaspoon baking powder

1 cup chopped walnuts

1 cup dark chocolate chips

1. Preheat the oven to 350°F.

2. Lightly grease a loaf pan with nonstick spray.

3. In a large mixing bowl, mash the bananas with a potato masher until almost smooth. Add the melted butter, eggs, sugar, and vanilla extract. Mix well to combine. Set aside.

4. In another bowl, add the salt, flour, baking soda, and baking powder. Mix well to combine, then add to the bowl with the mashed bananas. Add the chopped walnuts and chocolate and mix until well combined. Then pour the batter into the prepared loaf pan.

5. Bake in the preheated oven for 1 hour, or until a toothpick inserted into the center comes out clean.

6. Remove from the oven and let the bread sit on the counter for about 5 to 10 minutes. Then transfer the loaf to a wire rack and allow to cool completely before serving.

CHOCOLATE CHERRY SOURDOUGH

Here's a bread you're absolutely going to love. It's irresistibly chocolaty and fruity with enticing fragrances of roasted coffee. It's perfect for any time of year. Sure, the recipe contains a lot of repeated steps requiring you to fold the dough and wrap it in plastic wrap, but believe me, these redundant steps equal one terrific bread with time well spent in the kitchen. My biggest piece of advice is to not be afraid of baking bread. Worst case, you get a flat, misshapen loaf, but I promise it will still taste better than most storebought breads. Also, don't feel bad if you followed the recipe exactly and still didn't get beautiful results. Likely it's the temperature of your oven or maybe the flour or starter you're using. Just keep trying until you figure out what formula works best for you.

Makes 1 loaf

1 heaping teaspoon
   instant dry yeast

¾ cup warm water

1 cup + 1 tablespoon
   Sourdough Starter
   (page 54)

1⅔ cups bread flour, plus
   extra for dusting

¼ cup cocoa powder

1 tablespoon espresso or
   very strongly brewed
   coffee

1⅛ teaspoons fine salt

Canola oil (or other
   neutral oil), as needed,
   for greasing

1 cup dark chocolate chips

1 generous cup dried
   cherries

1. In a mixing bowl, add the yeast and water and whisk together. Allow the yeast to bloom, about 1 minute. Whisk in the Sourdough Starter until dissolved, then add the flour, cocoa powder, and coffee. Use a dough scraper to stir the ingredients together. Cover the bowl with plastic wrap and set aside for 20 minutes, then add the salt, incorporating it well. Transfer the sticky mixture to a lightly oiled plastic container and cover with plastic wrap.

2. Rest dough for 30 minutes, then lightly oil your hands to fold. Pull one edge of the dough up and press it down into the center of the ball. Repeat with the 3 other edges of the dough, then cover the dough. In 30 minutes, repeat the folding, this time incorporating the chocolate chips and cherries. Repeat the folding every half hour, for a total of 6 folds. Check the dough by pinching a piece between your fingers and stretching it. It should stretch out to a thin, transparent piece before tearing. If not, repeat folding and check again.

(Continued on next page)

3. Turn the bread out onto a lightly floured surface and use your hands to gently tuck the edges up toward the center of the dough, then flip the dough over so it's seam-side down, and gently round with your hands. Cover with plastic wrap and rest dough for 20 minutes, then tuck the edges down toward the seam to shape dough into a tighter ball. Cover with plastic wrap and rest for 10 minutes. Transfer to a flour-dusted wicker breadbasket, seam-side up, pinching the seam shut if necessary. Wrap basket with plastic wrap, or slide the basket into a clean plastic bag, closing it. Place in the refrigerator for 14 to 16 hours, or until dough has increased in size, and springs back slightly to the touch.

4. When you're ready to bake, remove the dough from the refrigerator and transfer it, smooth-side up, to a large cast-iron pot (with a lid) lined with a round of parchment paper. Be careful not to over-handle dough and lose air bubbles. Cover and bring to room temperature for 1 to 2 hours. Position a baking rack in the center of the oven and preheat to 500°F. Using a razor or fine, sharp knife blade, score a cross on the top of dough, making a fast, clean cut about $\frac{1}{8}$ to $\frac{1}{4}$ inch deep.

5. Bake covered for 33 minutes. Remove the lid and bake for another 10 minutes, cracking open the oven door for the last 5 minutes. Push a thermometer into the bread dough; it should read 195°F to 200°F degrees for cooked bread. Transfer the bread to a cooling rack, carefully remove the paper, and allow to cool completely at room temperature before slicing and serving.

DARK CHOCOLATE ZUCCHINI BREAD

If you love chocolate, like I do, you'll enjoy this deeply moist and fudgy bread that tastes like chocolate cake, but with the added subtle texture of zucchini. During the summer months, when my garden is overflowing with the abundant vegetable, I like to pick a few for this seasonal afternoon treat, which my family adores. This sumptuous recipe is easy, quick, and the results speak for themselves. I find the Dutch process cocoa powder is a must—the perfect accompaniment with chocolate chips. For the powder and chips, I prefer Hershey's, which is found in the baking section in most grocery stores.

Makes 1 loaf

2–3 small zucchinis

1¼ cups all-purpose flour

⅓ cup Dutch process cocoa powder

1 teaspoon baking soda

¼ teaspoon salt

¼ cup brown sugar

½ cup unsalted butter, melted

2 eggs

2 teaspoons vanilla extract

1 cup semi-sweet chocolate chips

1. Preheat the oven to 350°F.

2. Grease a 4½ × 8½–inch loaf pan. I like to use a nonstick baking spray. Then set aside. Note: You can also line the bottom of the pan with parchment or wax paper for easy removal after baking.

3. Wash the zucchini and trim off the ends. Use a box grater to grate the zucchinis (use the large grate), until you have approximately 1½ cups. Get two sheets of paper towel and place the grated zucchini between them and press out the excess water. You may need to do this a couple times to ensure the excess moisture is removed or you will end up with a soggy bread.

4. In a stand mixer with the paddle attachment, add to the mixing bowl the flour, cocoa powder, baking soda, salt, and brown sugar, then mix on low until incorporated. Then add the melted butter, eggs (one at a time), and vanilla extract. Continue to mix on low until you have a smooth, thick dough. Now, add the pressed zucchini and continue to mix on low until incorporated. Repeat with the chocolate chips.

(Continued on page 69)

5. Remove the dough mixture from the bowl and form into the prepared loaf pan. Place in the oven and bake until a clean toothpick comes out after inserted in the center, about 50 minutes to 1 hour. Note: The chocolate will be melted so when we talk about a clean toothpick, we're referring to the dough mixture, not the melted chocolate.

6. Remove the loaf and allow to cool on wire rack for about 15 minutes. Then invert, remove the loaf pan, and let the loaf cool another 15 more minutes before slicing and serving.

LEMON BARS

If you like lemon, you're going to find these lemon bars irresistible. The recipe is ridiculously easy, and the flavors are so bright and zingy with all that natural lemon flavor from the juice and zest. As you'll notice, I added the word *natural* in front of the lemon because the key with these bars is using fresh lemons. Remember, lemons are the star ingredient, so you don't want to use concentrate or bottled versions. Also, don't worry if your bars seem not quite done when you pull them from the oven. They will continue to set as they cool.

BARS:

½ cup cold butter

1 cup + 2 tablespoons all-purpose flour, divided

¼ cup powdered sugar

1 cup granulated sugar

½ teaspoon baking powder

2 eggs

1 lemon, juiced and zested

GLAZE:

2 tablespoons fresh lemon juice

¾ cup powdered sugar

1. Preheat the oven to 350°F.

2. In a mixing bowl, add the butter, 1 cup flour, and powdered sugar and cut together until incorporated. Then, using your fingers, press the crust mixture into an 8 × 8–inch pan.

3. Place the pan in the preheated oven and bake the crust for 15 minutes. Then remove.

4. In another mixing bowl, add the remaining 2 tablespoons flour along with the sugars and baking powder. Mix well until combined and then add the eggs, lemon juice, and lemon zest. Mix well to combine then pour the mixture into the baked crust. Place the pan back in the oven and bake for 20 to 25 minutes, or until the edges are golden brown and the mixture is set.

5. In the meantime, make the glaze, if desired. (If not desired, simply sprinkle with the powdered sugar!) Mix the lemon juice and powdered sugar until smooth.

6. Remove the bars from the oven and drizzle the glaze over them while they're still warm. Let the bars cool before cutting and serving.

LEMON CUSTARD CAKE

Here's a light and creamy, pudding-like cake that's quick and easy to make. The key to this soft and moist custard cake, like my Lemon Bars (page 70), is its bright and citrusy lemon flavor. That means always use fresh lemons, never concentrate, or bottled versions. The result is a melt-in-your-mouth dessert that everyone will love.

Makes 1 (8 × 8–inch) cake

4 eggs, separated

¾ cup sugar

½ cup unsalted butter, melted and cooled slightly

1 teaspoon pure vanilla extract

¾ cup all-purpose flour

¼ cup fresh lemon juice (about 2 lemons)

1¾ cups lukewarm milk

Powdered sugar, as needed, for dusting

1. Preheat the oven to 325°F.

2. Line an 8 × 8-inch baking dish with parchment paper, leaving overhang along the sides. Lightly grease with cooking spray and set aside.

3. In a mixing bowl, whip the egg whites until stiff peaks form and set aside. In another bowl, beat the egg yolks and sugar until pale yellow. Add the melted butter and vanilla and mix until combined. Add the flour and mix until evenly incorporated. Add the lemon juice and mix until combined. Slowly beat in the milk until well combined. Next, add the egg whites and whisk by hand. Don't fold in completely; leave some small egg white lumps. When you pour the batter into the pan, the lumps will float to the surface and create the top layer during baking.

4. Pour the thin batter into the pan and bake for 40 to 60 minutes, checking after 35 minutes, until the cake is barely jiggly in the center but the top is firm to the touch. Baking time might vary depending on your oven. Do not overbake or the cake will turn out rubbery and not custardy in the center. Once the cake has cooled, dust with the powdered sugar and serve.

PUMPKIN SQUARES WITH CREAM CHEESE FROSTING

When the leaves begin to drop and the weather starts getting colder, I'll make this fall classic—a perfect holiday treat for the entire family. The pumpkin squares are soft and moist and feature a thick layer of cream cheese frosting. You can serve these right away or, as I like to do, refrigerate them, and serve them cold.

Makes 12 to 18 squares

PUMPKIN SQUARES:

4 eggs

2 cups granulated sugar

1 cup vegetable oil

1 (15-ounce) can pumpkin purée

2 cups all-purpose flour

2 teaspoons baking soda

1 teaspoon cinnamon

½ teaspoon nutmeg

½ teaspoon ground ginger

½ teaspoon salt

CREAM CHEESE FROSTING:

8 ounces softened cream cheese

8 ounces softened butter

2 cups powdered sugar

1 teaspoon pure vanilla extract

1. Preheat oven to 350°F.

2. Grease a 9 × 13–inch baking pan and set aside. In a large bowl, add the eggs, sugar, oil, and pumpkin. Mix until well combined. In a separate bowl, add the flour, baking soda, cinnamon, nutmeg, ginger, and salt. Whisk until combined. Then add the "dry" ingredients to the "wet" egg mixture and gently stir until well combined. Pour batter into greased pan, then bake for 28 to 30 minutes or until a toothpick inserted in the middle comes out clean.

3. To make the frosting, using a standing kitchen mixer, beat the cream cheese and butter on high until smooth. Beat in the powdered sugar and vanilla until smooth and fluffy. Do not overbeat.

4. Remove from the oven and allow to cool completely. Once cooled, spread the Cream Cheese Frosting on top, cut into squares, and serve.

RED VELVET CUPCAKES
WITH CREAM CHEESE FROSTING

These deliciously festive, rich, and flavorful cupcakes stem from the classic red velvet cake, a true Southern classic. A dollop of tangy cream cheese frosting caps off the cupcakes for a delectable treat any time of year. Because we're using a little food coloring, be careful when putting this recipe together, as the batter can stain.

Makes 24 cupcakes

2½ cups flour

1½ cups sugar

1 teaspoon baking soda

1 tablespoon cocoa powder

1 teaspoon salt

2 large eggs

1½ cups vegetable oil

1 cup buttermilk

2 tablespoons (1 ounce) red food coloring

1 teaspoon pure vanilla extract

1 teaspoon white distilled vinegar

Red sugar crystals, or other decorative topping, as needed, for garnish

CREAM CHEESE FROSTING:

8 ounces softened cream cheese

8 ounces softened butter

2 cups powdered sugar

1 teaspoon pure vanilla extract

1. Preheat the oven to 350°F.

2. Line a muffin tin with cupcake liners and set aside.

3. In a medium bowl, add the flour, sugar, baking soda, cocoa powder, and salt. Mix until well combined. In a large bowl of a standing kitchen mixer (hand mixer will work too), add the eggs, oil, buttermilk, food coloring, vanilla extract, and vinegar. Beat until well incorporated. Next, add the "dry" ingredients to the bowl and beat until smooth, about 2 minutes. Divide the batter evenly among the lined muffin cups, filling about ¾ of the way. Bake for 16 to 18 minutes, or until a toothpick inserted in the centers comes out clean.

4. To make the frosting, using a standing kitchen mixer, beat the cream cheese and butter on high until smooth. Beat in the powdered sugar and vanilla until smooth and fluffy. Do not overbeat.

5. Remove from the oven and allow to cool completely before frosting and decorating with your favorite toppings. I prefer red sugar crystals.

WALNUT BANANA BREAD

This is one of my favorite afternoon snacks when the weather is blustery and cold outside. Enjoying a slice of soft, moist bread embraced by the creaminess of banana, the delicious crunch of walnuts, and all that chocolate flavor makes me feel all cozy inside, especially when accompanied by a hot cup of coffee. The winter spices of nutmeg and cinnamon elevate this bread even further. The next time you find yourself nestled at home with family and friends, try this comforting, decadent, and flavorful Walnut Banana Bread.

Makes 1 loaf

1½ cups all-purpose
   flour
1 pinch nutmeg
1 pinch cinnamon
1 teaspoon baking soda
¼ teaspoon salt
1½ cups mashed
   banana (3-4 overripe
   bananas)
6 tablespoons unsalted
   butter, melted and
   slightly cooled
¾ cup sugar
1 egg
1 teaspoon vanilla
   extract
1 cup chopped walnuts
1 cup dark or semi-sweet
   chocolate chips

1. Preheat the oven to 350°F.

2. Grease a 4½ × 8½–inch loaf pan. I like to use a nonstick baking spray. Then set aside. Note: You can also line the bottom of the pan with parchment or wax paper for easy removal after baking.

3. In a medium mixing bowl, whisk together the flour, nutmeg, cinnamon, baking soda, and salt until thoroughly combined. Set aside.

4. In a separate bowl, mix the mashed banana, melted butter, sugar, egg, and vanilla extract.

5. Slowly add the dry ingredients to the "wet" ingredients, and fold in until just combined. Then fold in the walnuts and chocolate chips.

6. Transfer the mixture into the prepared loaf pan and bake in the oven until golden brown and a toothpick comes out clean, about 50 minutes to 1 hour. Do not overbake. Note: The chocolate will be melted so when we talk about a clean toothpick, we're referring to the dough mixture, not the melted chocolate.

7. Remove from the oven and allow to cool on a wire rack before slicing and serving.

SNICKERDOODLE LOAF

My family loves when I make this Snickerdoodle Loaf, and I'm sure your family will enjoy it, too. You really can't go wrong with a cinnamon and sugar-laden bread, which is a very similar version of the Snickerdoodle cookie. If you can bake banana bread, you can bake this delicious loaf. The bread also freezes well in the rare case there are leftovers.

Makes 1 loaf

1½ cups all-purpose flour

1 teaspoon baking powder

½ teaspoon salt

1 teaspoon + ½ tablespoon cinnamon, divided

½ cup softened butter

1 cup sugar

2 eggs

1 teaspoon pure vanilla extract

½ cup plain Greek yogurt

1 teaspoon brown sugar

1. Preheat oven to 350°F.

2. Lightly spray a loaf pan and set aside.

3. In a medium bowl, add the flour, baking powder, salt, and 1 teaspoon of cinnamon. Mix well until combined. In a large bowl, add the butter and sugar and, using an electric mixer, beat until fluffy. Then add the eggs, vanilla, and Greek yogurt. Mix well to combine. Add the "dry" ingredients and stir until just combined. Pour the batter into the prepared pan.

4. Next, in a small dish, add the brown sugar and remaining ½ tablespoon of cinnamon. Mix well to combine and top the bread evenly with the mixture.

5. Bake in the preheated oven for 50 minutes, or until the bread is golden brown on top and a toothpick inserted in the center comes out clean. Remove the bread from the oven and allow to cool for 10 minutes, then transfer to a wire rack to continue cooling before serving.

BLUE CHEESE AND WALNUT PULL-APART BREAD

If you're a fan of blue cheese, you're in for a real treat with this blue cheese-stuffed bread that's also baked with crunchy walnuts and Parmesan then topped with fresh thyme and seasoned with salt and pepper. This bread is delicious and pairs well with any hot sauced or spicy chicken dish.

Makes 1 pastry wheel

2 tablespoons honey

2 sheets puff pastry squares

¼ cup chopped walnuts

½ cup crumbled blue cheese

½ cup grated Parmesan cheese

6 sprigs fresh thyme, leaves chopped

Sea salt and fresh cracked black pepper, as needed, to taste

1 tablespoon whole milk

1. Preheat the oven to 350°F.

2. Drizzle 1 tablespoon of honey on each sheet of puff pastry. Divide the walnuts, blue cheese, and Parmesan cheese and scatter over each sheet of puff pastry. Top each sheet with fresh thyme leaves and season with sea salt and cracked pepper.

3. Roll up each sheet of pastry and cut in half lengthways. Note: You may need to tuck in the pastry after cutting to keep the filling inside.

4. On a sheet of baking paper, carefully twist each length of pastry and make a round coil shape. Brush with milk and bake in the oven for 25 to 30 minutes, or until the pastry is puffed and golden and cooked through.

5. Remove from the oven, scatter extra thyme leaves over the top, and serve warm.

CHEESY SPINACH DAMPER

Damper is a savory Australian bread and one of my favorites to make during the colder months of the year. That's because there's nothing better than a warm, fresh-out-of-the-oven loaf that's light and fluffy and extremely moist with a cheesy-garlicky inside that complements the crumbly outer crust. I made this damper at a holiday party recently, and everybody was amazed at how light and delicious it was. This recipe makes one loaf, which can be served as a hearty side dish or cut into smaller pieces to feed a crowd.

Makes 1 loaf

2½ cups all-purpose flour

¾ cup unsalted butter (¼ cup cold; ½ cup softened), cubed, divided

1½ cups spinach leaves, chopped

1 cup whole milk + more to brush

1 garlic clove, peeled and minced

1¼ cups grated sharp cheddar, divided

1 teaspoon finely chopped fresh rosemary

1. Preheat oven to 400°F.

2. Line a baking sheet with a silicone sheet or parchment paper.

3. In a food processor, add the flour and ¼ cup of the butter. Mix for 10 to 20 seconds, or until the mixture resembles fine crumbs. Add the spinach, milk, garlic, and 1 cup of the cheddar cheese. Mix until the mixture comes together in a soft dough. Use damp hands to transfer to a well-floured surface. Knead until smooth, then shape into a thick disc with smooth sides. Place on the prepared sheet. Use a lightly floured knife to score 8 wedges, about ½ inch deep.

4. Brush the dough with a little milk and sprinkle with remaining ¼ cup cheddar cheese.

5. Bake in the preheated oven for 25 to 30 minutes, or until golden brown and the bottom sounds hollow when tapped. Remove from oven.

6. In a small bowl, add the ½ cup softened butter along with the rosemary. Mix to combine and serve alongside the warm damper.

CLASSIC BISCUITS

If you enjoy soft, buttery biscuits made from scratch, you'll appreciate these simple biscuits. Best of all, they're made with butter—no shortening—and other easy-to-find pantry ingredients. That means you can make delicious biscuits at home without having to buy premade biscuits, which never taste as good and are usually filled with preservatives and artificial flavors. When making these biscuits, technique is important, so take your time when assembling to ensure you turn out a perfect biscuit each and every time.

Makes 8 biscuits

6 tablespoons unsalted butter

2 cups all-purpose flour

1 tablespoon sugar

¼ teaspoon baking soda

1 tablespoon baking powder

1 teaspoon salt

1 cup cold buttermilk

Melted butter, as needed, for brushing

1. Begin by cutting the butter into small cubes. Place the butter on a plate and transfer to the freezer. Next, line a baking sheet with a silicone sheet or parchment paper and set aside.

2. Preheat the oven to 450°F.

3. In a food processor, add the flour, sugar, baking soda, baking powder, and salt. Pulse a time or two to combine. Add the cold butter to the food processor and pulse to combine. The butter should be no larger than the size of a pea when you're done.

4. Add the butter and flour mixture to a large bowl and make a well in the middle. Add the cold buttermilk. Stir until the dough is mixed and combined, slightly sticky to the touch. If the dough is too sticky, add a little flour to the mixture until it's only *slightly* sticky to the touch.

5. Next, turn out the dough onto a floured surface and pat into a rectangle about 8 to 9 inches long. Gently fold the right side of the dough toward the middle, then fold the left side in toward the middle, as well. It should look like a trifold paper. Now rotate the dough a quarter turn (it should be horizontal), and pat down into an 8- to 9-inch-long rectangle again. Repeat the folding technique from the step above, at least one or two more times. The more

(Continued on page 85)

folding you do, the more layers you'll have. Finally, pat dough down into a rectangle again, about 1-inch thick.

6. Using a 2½-inch-round biscuit cutter, push down to cut the dough and pull straight up (do not twist). Leftover scraps can be combined and cut again. Be careful not to overwork the dough or the biscuits won't be flaky.

7. Place the biscuits on the prepared baking sheet and bake in the preheated oven for 12 to 15 minutes, or until golden and cooked through. Remove from the oven and brush the tops with melted butter before serving.

CRUMPETS

This traditional British teatime treat is a cross between an English muffin and a pancake. Like a muffin, it's filled with holes, perfect to collect all that melted butter or jam smothered over the top. Crumpets are also moister and thinner, taking on a pancake-like texture. At home, I prefer to toast my crumpets until golden before serving. And since the holes on the crumpet reach the outside crust, there's no need to split them before toasting.

Makes 7 crumpets

1½ cups all-purpose flour plus more for dredging

1 teaspoon sugar

¾ teaspoon salt

½ teaspoon instant dry yeast

½ teaspoon baking soda

1⅓ cups very warm water

1. In a large bowl, combine the flour, sugar, salt, yeast, and baking soda. Add the warm water and use an electric mixer to beat for 1 minute. Cover the bowl with a clean towel or plate and set in a warm place for 30 to 45 minutes. The mixture should be frothy on top.

2. Next, grease the inside of 3 or 4 crumpet rings with a little butter and dip them in flour, tapping off the excess flour. Set aside.

3. Heat a large nonstick skillet over medium-high heat. Place 2 or 3 of the crumpet rings into the pan and fill each ring with about ¼ cup of the batter. Allow to cook for 5 to 6 minutes, or until there is a ring of dry batter and bubbles bursting around the edge of the crumpets. Reduce the heat to medium-low and cook for another 5 to 6 minutes, or until all the bubbles have stopped popping. Remove the rings and gently flip the crumpets over and cook for 2 or 3 seconds—just enough to seal the tops. Remove the crumpets from the pan and allow to cool. Clean the rings and re-grease and flour. Repeat the previous steps for the remaining batter until all the crumpets are cooked.

GOUGERES

Gougeres are a small, round puff pastry that's mixed with grated cheeses and herbs and baked until puffed, hollow, and soft on the inside—almost like a cream puff—while crisp and golden on the outside. Like the Spinach Ricotta Rolls (page 96), Gougeres make a great snack and should be served warm since they're full of cheese.

Makes 18 Gougeres

¾ cup water

5 tablespoons unsalted butter

½ teaspoon salt

⅛ teaspoon fresh cracked black pepper

1 cup all-purpose flour

4 eggs

¾ cup grated mozzarella cheese

¼ teaspoon minced flat leaf (Italian) parsley

½ cup grated Parmesan cheese

1. Preheat the oven to 425°F.

2. Line a baking sheet with a silicone sheet or parchment paper.

3. In a medium saucepan, add the water, butter, salt, and pepper and bring to a boil. Add the flour and stir until a dough forms. Cook another 2 minutes to dry the dough.

4. Transfer the dough to a bowl and let cool slightly. Slowly add the eggs, one at a time, stirring until well combined. Add the mozzarella cheese and parsley and mix well. Using 2 tablespoons, round each ball of dough and place onto the prepared parchment paper. Set them about 2 inches apart. Sprinkle some grated Parmesan cheese on top.

5. Bake in the preheated oven for 10 minutes, then reduce the oven temperature to 380°F. Bake an additional 20 to 25 minutes, or until golden brown. Remove from the oven and serve warm.

JALAPEÑO BACON BREAD

When it comes to a delicious and versatile bread, this one is often my go-to. That's because this savory Jalapeño Bacon Bread can be served as a sandwich bread, soup dipper, or afternoon snack. Unlike most breads, which require yeast and eggs, this bread uses neither. That means you can prepare this bread quickly and easily without having to worry about rising time and climate control, which is needed when making traditional yeast breads.

Makes 1 loaf

8 ounces cream cheese, softened

¼ cup diced jalapeño (with seeds if you like extra heat)

2 cups cooked, chopped bacon

2 cups cheddar cheese

3 cups all-purpose flour

1 tablespoon baking powder

1 teaspoon salt

2 tablespoons granulated sugar

1 tablespoon vegetable oil

1½ cups buttermilk

1. Preheat the oven 350°F.

2. Grease a 5 × 9–inch loaf pan with nonstick spray or butter.

3. In a large bowl, add the cream cheese, jalapeños, bacon, and cheese. Stir to combine. In another bowl, add the flour, baking powder, salt, and sugar. Mix to combine. Now add the cream cheese mixture to the flour mixture, along with the vegetable oil and buttermilk. Mix until just combined.

4. Pour the batter into loaf pan and transfer to the preheated oven. Bake for 50 to 55 minutes, or until the top is browned and a toothpick comes out clean when inserted into the center.

5. Remove the loaf from the oven and place on a wire rack to cool for about 5 minutes before serving.

ROSEMARY FOCACCIA

I love homemade focaccias, and this one is no exception—a soft and fluffy focaccia topped with fresh rosemary, olive oil, and kosher salt. Focaccias are easy to make by hand and even easier with the help of a kitchen mixer. In the winter, the dough may take a little longer to rise due to the cold ambient temperature, and during the summer, it may rise quicker. It's important to make sure the dough doubles in size or you won't yield a light fluffy loaf. I like using a cast-iron skillet for a satisfyingly chewy crust, but a baking sheet works just as well.

Makes 1 loaf

1⅓ cups very warm water

2 teaspoons sugar

1 (0.25-ounce) package active-dry yeast

3½ cups all-purpose flour

¼ cup extra virgin olive oil, plus more for drizzling

2 teaspoons kosher salt, plus more for finishing

2 sprigs fresh rosemary, chopped

1. Add the warm water and sugar to the bowl of a standing mixer (or large bowl) with the dough attachment. Stir to combine, then sprinkle the yeast on top of the water and stir again to combine. Let sit for 5 to 10 minutes until the yeast is foamy.

2. Next, set the mixer to low speed. Working in small batches, add the flour, olive oil, and salt. Increase the speed to medium-low and continue mixing the dough for 5 minutes. If the dough is too sticky and isn't pulling away from the sides of the bowl, add in an extra ¼ cup flour while mixing.

3. Remove the dough from the mixing bowl and use your hands to shape into a ball. Grease the mixing bowl with cooking spray, then place the dough back into the bowl and cover with a damp towel. Place in a warm location and let the dough rise for 60 minutes, or until nearly doubled in size.

4. Turn the dough onto a floured surface and roll into a large circle or rectangle until the dough is about ½ inch thick. Cover the dough again with a damp towel and let rise for another 20 minutes.

(Continued on page 93)

5. Preheat oven to 400°F.

6. Before baking, use your fingers to poke deep dents all over the surface of the dough. Drizzle a tablespoon or two of olive oil evenly over the top of the dough and sprinkle with the fresh rosemary and kosher salt.

7. Bake for 20 minutes, or until the dough is slightly golden and cooked through.

8. Remove from the oven and drizzle with a little more olive oil, if desired. Let cool for 5 minutes, slice, and serve warm with good-quality olive oil and balsamic vinegar to dip.

TOMATO FOCACCIA

Tomato Focaccia is one of my best-loved bread recipes. It is a basic dough of few ingredients that yields a perfect golden crust. This native Italian bread recipe has acquired worldwide recognition for its magnificent taste and ease to make. Tomato Focaccia brims with mouth-watering rosemary aroma, robust tomato flavors, and an olive oil–based crunchiness that is unrivaled. I find using garden-fresh cherry tomatoes brings out the best in both the tomato and bread flavors. *Il gusto sapore di questo pane e' delizioso*—The taste of this bread is delicious.

Makes 1 loaf

4 cups all-purpose flour

2¼ teaspoons instant yeast

2 teaspoons kosher salt, plus more for sprinkling

2 tablespoons chopped fresh rosemary leaves, plus more for sprinkling

2 cups warm water

⅓ cup extra virgin olive oil, divided

1 pint cherry tomatoes, halved

Sea salt, as needed

1. In the bowl of a stand mixer, add the flour, yeast, salt, and rosemary. Mix on low to combine. With the mixer on low, add the water and 2 tablespoons of the olive oil. Mix until a soft wet dough forms. Note: It will be very sticky.

2. Cover and let rise in a warm place for 40 minutes to 1 hour.

3. Preheat the oven to 425°F.

4. Turn the dough out onto a well-oiled half sheet pan, or line the pan with parchment paper or a silicone mat. Use your fingers to press out the dough into a large rectangle within the pan.

5. Place the remaining olive oil in a small bowl and dip your fingers into the oil, then poke little indents all over the bread, leaving little pools of oil. Do this all over the surface.

6. Arrange the tomatoes across the top, cut-side up, pressing them into the dough slightly, then scatter more chopped rosemary leaves evenly across the surface. Sprinkle sea salt over the dough.

7. Bake for 35 to 40 minutes, or until golden and crusty.

8. Remove the bread from the pan and let cool on a rack before cutting into wedges and serving.

SPINACH RICOTTA ROLLS

When I'm looking for a great finger food or snack to satisfy my family and friends, these savory rolls filled with the classic spinach and ricotta cheese combination are the answer. The rolls are easy to make and the buttery, flaky, fluffy pastry is the perfect vessel to house the juicy, cheesy filling inside. I like making a batch ahead of time and having the rolls ready on the counter to reheat at a moment's notice.

Makes 20 rolls

DOUGH:

1 cup whole milk, warmed

1 teaspoon sugar

1 tablespoon instant yeast

3¼ cups all-purpose flour, plus extra for dusting

1 tablespoon salt

1 egg

2 tablespoons olive oil

FILLING:

1 cup ricotta cheese

2 eggs, divided

½ teaspoon minced garlic

1 teaspoon salt

¼ teaspoon fresh cracked black pepper

½ teaspoon dried oregano

2 cups chopped spinach

1. Begin by making the dough. In a small bowl, add the warm milk, sugar, and yeast. Stir together until foamy, about 5 to 10 minutes.

2. Next, in the bowl of a standing kitchen mixer, add the flour and salt and mix.

3. In a separate bowl, add 1 egg and olive oil and beat well until combined. Make a well in the middle of the flour and pour the egg/olive oil mixture inside followed by the milk/yeast mixture. Using the dough hook attachment, stir the dough on low speed and gradually increase to medium speed. Stop to scrape the edges of the bowl, if necessary, and knead for 5 to 8 minutes. The dough should be smooth and stretchy. Cover the bowl with a kitchen towel and leave in a warm place to proof (about 1 hour or until doubled in size).

4. To make the filling, in a large bowl, add the ricotta cheese and 1 egg and mix until combined. Stir in the garlic, salt, pepper, and oregano. Thinly chop the spinach and add to the ricotta filling. Mix until fully incorporated and set aside.

5. To make the rolls, punch the dough to remove any air then transfer to a lightly floured surface. Using a rolling pin, roll the dough into a large thin rectangle. Spread the ricotta and spinach filling over the rolled dough, leaving one of the longest side clean. Roll the dough on its longest side, then cut small rolls (about 2 inches thick). Place the rolls on a baking tray lined with a silicone mat or parchment paper and leave to proof for 30 minutes.

6. Preheat the oven on 350°F.

7. In a small bowl, beat the remaining egg with a little water to create an egg wash. Using a pastry brush, brush a little bit of egg wash over each roll.

8. Bake for 15 to 20 minutes, then set aside to cool. Serve warm.

MID-DAY SNACKS

We've all had that mid-day slump, especially at the office, when our eyes begin to water, we yawn more than usual, and our focus is a bit less than we want it to be. Don't worry any longer—I've got the best remedy.

Does your body crave something sweet? Take a quick visit to the home or office kitchen for an energy-packed slice of Chocolate Zucchini Brownie (page 103) or a piece of creamy, rich, antioxidant-laden Blueberry Cream Cheese Babka (page 100). You could also opt for a good dose of carbs with my delicious Gingerbread Pudding (page 109) while enjoying a slice of my Pumpkin Bread with Cinnamon Streusel (page 111) will bring your senses back to full focus.

Does your body want an energy-boosting savory snack? Grab a handful of Pretzel Bites and a bit of Cheddar Cheese Sauce (page 117), heat them up, and snack away. A power-packed afternoon munchie is what you will find with my Pumpkin, Spinach, Zucchini, and Cheddar Muffins (page 120). These muffins are a wonderful food to nibble on plain or with some butter. Two recipes that fit the bill for late-afternoon healthy snacking are my Roasted Red Pepper Phyllo Quiche Bites (page 121) and a lovely slice of traditional Spanakopita (page 122). These will certainly please the palate and fill the requirement of a healthy snack.

Enjoy the mid-day recipes on the following pages, as they will help keep your mind and body in tiptop shape to get you through the rest of the afternoon.

BLUEBERRY CREAM CHEESE BABKA

Babkas have a rich history that originated in traditional Eastern European bakeries. They can be either sweet or savory with a dough similar to that of croissants. Blueberries and cream cheese are a traditional sweet filling; yet I sometimes like to use raspberry preserves to change it up a bit. When I want to serve this with a breakfast or brunch meal, I prepare the dough the evening before and let it rise in the refrigerator overnight. In the morning, I finish with the last few steps to allow the fresh-baked babka smells to fill the kitchen. The time spent on this aromatic sweet bread is well worth it—guaranteed to please family and friends with each bite.

Makes 2 loaves

BLUEBERRY PRESERVES:

3 cups fresh blueberries

¾ cup granulated sugar

1 tablespoon fresh lemon juice

CREAM CHEESE FILLING:

1 (8-ounce) package cream cheese, softened

½ cup granulated sugar

BABKA DOUGH:

4 cups all-purpose flour

⅓ cup granulated sugar + 1 teaspoon, divided

1 teaspoon kosher salt

1 cup warm whole milk

2¼ teaspoons active dry yeast

2 eggs

1. Begin by making the Blueberry Preserves. In a medium saucepan over high heat, add the blueberries, sugar, and lemon juice. Bring to a boil, then reduce the heat to medium and simmer for about 15 minutes, stirring occasionally and crushing some of the blueberries with the back of the spoon, until thickened. Note: You can do this the day before to save time or do it when the dough is rising.

2. To make the Cream Cheese Filling, in a bowl add the cream cheese and sugar. Beat with an electric mixer until combined, then set aside until ready to fill the dough.

3. To make the Babka Dough, in a bowl of standing mixer fit with a dough hook, add the flour, ⅓ cup sugar, and salt. Whisk together then add the warm milk and remaining teaspoon of sugar. Sprinkle the yeast over the milk and stir to combine. Let stand for about 5 minutes until the yeast starts to foam, then add the eggs and vanilla. Mix on low speed until combined and then increase speed to medium low and mix for about 5 minutes until the dough is smooth. Add the softened butter 1 tablespoon at a time and mix on medium-low for about 4 minutes, or until the butter is incorporated and the dough comes together but

1 teaspoon pure
vanilla extract

¾ cup butter,
cubed, at room
temperature

SUGAR SYRUP:

⅓ cup granulated
sugar

⅓ cup water

is sticky. Scrape down the sides of the bowl as needed during mixing.

4. Cover the bowl with plastic wrap and let rise in a warm place for 1 to 1½ hours, or until the dough is about doubled (or let rise in the refrigerator overnight). Punch down the dough and scrape out onto a lightly floured surface. Divide the dough into 2 halves and shape into a rectangle. Starting with one disc, roll the dough out on a floured surface to a 12 × 16–inch rectangle. Spread half the cream cheese mixture, leaving a small border on one long edge. Then spread with half the blueberry preserves, again leaving a border on a long edge.

5. Starting with the long side without the border, roll the dough into a tight log. If the dough is very warm or sticky, you can refrigerate the dough for about 30 minutes to make it easier to work with (if you didn't refrigerate overnight). Trim off about 1 inch from each side. Slice the dough down the middle lengthwise into 2 long halves with the layers exposed. Place the end of one of the halves over the top of the other half, pressing together lightly and then braid the 2 pieces over one another to the bottom, again pressing together lightly. Repeat the last two steps with the other dough disc.

6. Line two, 9 × 5–inch loaf pans with parchment paper, leaving an overhang on the long sides. Carefully place the braided dough into each loaf pan, squeezing the ends slightly to fit if needed. Cover with plastic wrap and let rise in a warm place for an hour.

7. Make the Sugar Syrup by adding the sugar and water in a small saucepan over medium-high heat. Stir frequently until the sugar is dissolved. Set aside to cool.

8. Bake the dough at 350°F for about 40 minutes or until golden brown and a toothpick inserted in the center comes out clean. Immediately after taking out of the oven, brush each loaf with the Sugar Syrup, using it all. Cool a few minutes in the loaf pan and then transfer the babka using the parchment paper to a wire rack to cool completely.

CHOCOLATE ZUCCHINI BROWNIES

Here's another one of those recipes with a name that disguises its culinary appeal and amazing taste. Zucchini and brownies may sound like an oxymoron, but I assure you they aren't. Other perfectly paired zucchini partners include zucchini and banana bread, zucchini and cinnamon coffee cake, and blueberry zucchini squares. Each bite of my Chocolate Zucchini Brownie is a decadent gorging of flavors and aromas. So, take a walk on the wild side, be unpredictable with your culinary imagination, and move this wonderfully moist brownie recipe to the top of your things-to-bake list. You will not regret it.

Makes 24 brownies

2 cups all-purpose flour
½ cup unsweetened cocoa powder
1½ teaspoons baking soda
1 teaspoon salt
½ cup vegetable oil
1½ cups granulated sugar
2 teaspoons pure vanilla extract
2 cups shredded zucchini (pressed in paper towel to extract excess water)
3–5 tablespoons water
Semisweet chocolate chips, for garnish, optional

1. Preheat oven to 350°F.

2. Line a 9 × 13–inch baking pan with foil and spray with cooking spray. Set aside.

3. In a medium bowl, add the flour, cocoa, baking soda, and salt. Whisk together until incorporated and set aside.

4. Using an electric mixer fitted with a paddle attachment, pour in the oil, sugar, and vanilla, and mix well until combined. Add in the "dry" ingredients and stir. Fold in the zucchini. Let the mixture sit for several minutes so the batter can absorb the moisture from the zucchini. Note: If the mixture is powdery, add up to 5 tablespoons of water. Start with 1 tablespoon and work up from there, stirring well after each addition. The batter should be thick and not powdery. Spread the dough in the prepared pan. Sprinkle the top with chocolate chips, if desired.

5. Bake 25 for 30 minutes, or until the brownies spring back when gently touched. Remove from the oven and let cool slightly before serving.

CHOCOLATE ZUCCHINI BUNDT CAKE

When my summer garden offers a bounty of zucchini, I often turn to this recipe as a delicious alternative to the popular zucchini bread. Remember, when you are preparing the Bundt pan, use an oil-based product, not butter. The milk solids in the butter can solidify when baked and make the cake stick to the pan. The double whammy of chocolate in this wonderful recipe—in the cake and in the icing—make this an ideal dessert for your favorite chocolate lover.

Makes 1 cake

CAKE:
¾ cup unsalted butter, softened
½ cup granulated sugar
½ cup brown sugar
3 large eggs
2 teaspoons pure vanilla extract
2½ cups all-purpose flour
½ cup Dutch process cocoa powder

2 teaspoons baking powder
1 teaspoon baking soda
1 teaspoon salt
½ teaspoon ground cinnamon
¼ teaspoon nutmeg
½ cup buttermilk
3 cups finely shredded zucchini, pressed to release excess water
1 cup chocolate chips

GLAZE:
1¼ cups semisweet chocolate chips
½ cup heavy whipping cream
2 tablespoons mini chocolate chips

1. Preheat the oven to 350°F.

2. Grease a Bundt pan with cooking spray.

3. In a stand mixer, add the butter and sugars and mix until creamy. Add the eggs and vanilla and mix again. In a separate mixing bowl, add the flour, cocoa powder, baking powder, baking soda, salt, cinnamon, and nutmeg. Mix well and then add to the mixer along with the buttermilk. Mix until well incorporated. Stir in the zucchini and chocolate chips by hand, then pour the mixture into the prepared pan.

4. Transfer the pan to the preheated oven for 50 to 60 minutes, or until a toothpick inserted into the center comes out clean. Remove from the oven and let cool in the pan for 15 minutes, then flip the cake out onto a plate and let cool completely.

5. To make the glaze, in a microwave-safe bowl, add the chocolate chips and whipping cream. Heat for about 30 seconds. Stir until melted and creamy. Let cool 5 to 10 minutes, then spoon over the top of the cake. Sprinkle with the mini chocolate chips, slice, and serve.

CINNAMON ROLL COFFEE CAKE

Was this from scratch? That's the question you'll receive when you serve this scrumptious, all-time favorite coffee cake. Far outperforming any box mix or pop-out-of-a-can dough, this recipe is delightfully simple and can be easily made in the morning before breakfast. Hey—it can, in a pinch, be made before dinner so there is a fresh-baked dessert cake to serve with coffee after dinner. Any leftovers can be reheated.

Servers 12

CAKE:

½ cup melted butter

2 large eggs

1 cup granulated sugar

3 cups all-purpose flour

2 teaspoons pure vanilla extract

4 teaspoons baking powder

¼ teaspoon salt

1½ cups whole milk

TOPPING:

1 cup melted butter

1 cup brown sugar

2 tablespoons flour

1 tablespoon ground cinnamon

GLAZE:

2 cups powdered sugar

5 tablespoons milk

1 teaspoon pure vanilla extract

1. Preheat oven to 350°

2. In a large bowl, mix all the cake ingredients together until well combined. Pour into a greased 9 × 13–inch pan.

3. For the Topping, mix all the ingredients together in a small bowl until well combined. Spread evenly on the batter and swirl with a knife.

4. Bake at 350°F for 30 to 35 minutes.

5. For the Glaze, mix all the ingredients together in a small bowl until it is a consistency like pancake syrup. Drizzle glaze over cake while still warm.

6. Best served warm or room temperature.

S'MORES COOKIES

You don't need a campfire to make these family-favorite delights. I like to make a batch of S'mores Cookies to have at-the-ready after a day of cross-country skiing or a morning's winter hike. Tip: These cookies can be made ahead and then reheated for 3 minutes in a 400°F oven or about 1 minute in an air fryer. Chocolate lovers will enjoy the double hit of chocolate found both in the cookie and on top of the marshmallow.

Makes 4 dozen

1½ cups all-purpose flour

1 cup graham cracker crumbs

1 teaspoon baking soda

1 teaspoon salt

1 dash cinnamon

1 cup butter, softened

¾ cup sugar

¾ cup brown sugar

1 teaspoon vanilla extract

2 eggs

2 cups miniature chocolate chips

1½ cups mini marshmallows

2 Hershey's bars, chopped

1. Preheat oven to 375°F.

2. In a medium bowl, combine the flour, graham cracker crumbs, baking soda, salt, and dash of cinnamon.

3. In a large bowl, beat together the butter, sugar, brown sugar, and vanilla extract until creamy. Add the eggs one at a time until well mixed. Slowly beat in the flour mixture until smooth. Stir in the chocolate chips.

4. Drop by rounded tablespoon onto ungreased cookie sheet. Bake for 8 minutes and remove from the oven. Push 3 to 4 marshmallows and a few pieces of Hershey bar into each cookie. Return to the oven and bake an additional 3 to 4 minutes until fully cooked. Cool cookies on a wire rack.

GINGERBREAD PUDDING

The sweet-savory aroma of this delicious bread pudding fills my kitchen as it is baking. This favorite smell is one that wakes up the senses and gets my family ready for the day. After all, breakfast is one of the most important meals—so why not start with a savory bread? Or, if you'd like, this is also a lovely dessert to serve either with a Sunday brunch or after dinner. The combination of the brioche bread's mildly sweet flavor with lemon and butter blends perfectly with the deep, rich flavors of molasses and ginger. If you can't find brioche bread, a comparable substitute is challah or Portuguese sweet bread.

Serves 10 to 12

1 loaf brioche bread, cut into
   1-inch chunks
2½ cups whole milk
5 eggs
⅔ cup brown sugar
¼ cup molasses
1 teaspoon ginger
1½ teaspoons ground cinnamon
½ teaspoon nutmeg
½ teaspoon allspice
1 teaspoon pure vanilla extract

SAUCE:
1½ cups granulated sugar
1½ sticks unsalted butter,
   slightly melted
1 (14-ounce) can sweetened
   condensed milk
1 egg yolk
2 teaspoons pure vanilla extract

1. Preheat the oven to 350°F.

2. Place bread on baking sheet and place in oven for about 10 minutes, turning halfway through to crisp the bread up. Prepare casserole dish with cooking spray. Remove toasted bread from oven and put directly into prepared casserole dish.

3. In a medium bowl combine milk, eggs, sugar, molasses, spices, and vanilla and whisk until combined. Pour over your bread and stir until absorbed, let sit for about 10 to 15 minutes. Place in preheated oven and bake for about 45 to 60 minutes or until center is set and no longer runny.

4. While the pudding is cooling slightly, add to a saucepan your sugar, butter, and sweetened condensed milk and stir until combined. Cook over medium-high heat until melted and creamy. Remove from heat.

5. In large bowl, beat your egg, add a little bit of the sauce at a time to temper the egg so it doesn't scramble, and whisk together. Stir in the vanilla. Pour over your bread pudding and serve warm.

PUMPKIN BREAD WITH CINNAMON STREUSEL

This moist and spicy bread is complemented by the delightfully sweet and crunchy topping. A shortcut for removing the loaf from the pan is to use parchment paper. Use enough of it to have the paper hang off the sides for easy removal after baking. There's no getting around the savory aroma of pumpkin bread while it is baking.

Makes 1 loaf

BATTER:

½ cup unsalted butter, at room temperature

1 cup granulated sugar

½ cup light brown sugar

1 egg

1 teaspoon pure vanilla extract

¼ cup sour cream

1 cup pumpkin

1½ cups all-purpose flour

¾ teaspoon salt

2 teaspoons baking powder

1½ teaspoons cinnamon

⅛ teaspoon ground cloves

STREUSEL TOPPING:

¼ cup melted unsalted butter

2 tablespoons light brown sugar

1 teaspoon ground cinnamon

1 cup +/- 1 tablespoon all-purpose flour

¼ cup pecans chopped

1. Preheat oven to 350°F.

2. Grease a standard loaf pan with cooking spray.

3. In a stand mixer, add the butter and sugars together and mix until combined. Add the egg, vanilla, sour cream, and pumpkin and mix until well combined. In a medium bowl, add the flour, salt, baking powder, cinnamon, and cloves and mix. Slowly add the "dry" ingredients to the mixer while running on low. Mix until a thick batter forms, then place the batter into the loaf pan.

4. To make the Streusel Topping, in a small bowl add the melted butter, brown sugar, and cinnamon and mix until smooth. Slowly add the flour into the mixture and mix until crumbly. Note: You may need to add a little extra flour if the mixture is too wet.

5. Sprinkle the streusel and chopped pecans over the pumpkin bread batter. Transfer to the preheated oven and bake for 60 to 70 minutes, or until a toothpick comes out clean. Remove from the oven and cool slightly before serving.

THIN MINT COOKIES

Who doesn't smile and think of Girl Scout cookies when hearing or reading about Thin Mint Cookies? This is a simple recipe to make these melt-in-your mouth, family-favorite cookies all year round. I like the Dutch process cocoa as it has a more intense chocolate flavor than natural cocoa powder. Also, it's important to make sure the dough is very cold before rolling it out to a thin layer. I often make this recipe and freeze some Thin Mints just for those times when I need a sweet treat when visitors stop by.

Makes 4 dozen

COOKIES:

2 sticks unsalted butter, room temperature

1 cup powdered sugar

¾ teaspoon salt

1 teaspoon pure vanilla extract

1 cup unsweetened Dutch cocoa powder

1½ cups all-purpose flour

PEPPERMINT COATING:

2 cups semi-sweet baking chocolate

1 teaspoon coconut oil

1 teaspoon peppermint extract

1. Preheat the oven to 350°F.

2. Prepare two baking sheets and line with silicone mat or parchment paper.

3. Cream butter until light and fluffy, then add the powdered sugar and mix until combined. Stir in the salt, vanilla, and cocoa powder. Mix until the cocoa powder is integrated, and the batter resembles a thick frosting. Add the flour and mix just until the flour is combined, making sure to not overmix. Form dough into a ball. Knead a few times to bring together, then flatten into a disc between ½ inch and 1 inch thick, cover in plastic wrap, and place in freezer for 15 minutes. Remove dough from the freezer and roll it out thin on a floured surface, about ⅛ inch. Cut cookies using 1½-inch cutter (or a shot glass works in a pinch).

4. Place cookies on a baking sheet and bake for 10 minutes. Remove the cookies from the oven and allow them to cool completely on a wire rack. While the cookies bake, make the Peppermint Coating. Chop the baking chocolate into very small, thin pieces. Place in a glass measuring cup or similar container along with the oil and microwave in short 15- to 20-second bursts. Add peppermint extract.

5. Gently drop the cookies, one at a time, into the coating. Turn to coat entirely, then lift the cookie out of the chocolate with the fork and tap the fork (with the cookie on top) on the side of the pan until the extra coating drips off. Place on a parchment or plastic wrap-lined baking sheet and repeat for the rest of the cookies. You may want to put them in the fridge for a few minutes before serving to harden the coating, but it's not necessary.

BALSAMIC MUSHROOM TARTS

I know mushrooms may not be a popular ingredient in pastry recipes, but take a leap of faith with this recipe and you'll love these savory open-faced Balsamic Mushroom Tarts. The flaky pastry, balsamic caramelized mushrooms with shallots, garlic, and thyme, topped with the deep flavor of Gruyère cheese, help to add a wonderful savory taste to the puff pastry–based dish. This recipe can be a starter before a main entrée, a snack while watching a good movie, or the perfect finger food at a family home party or social gathering. Don't miss the opportunity to explore your culinary experiences and give these pastry tartlets a go.

Makes 10 tarts

7 ounces good-quality puff pastry dough, cut into 2 rectangles

5 ounces grated Gruyère cheese, plus extra for sprinkling

3 tablespoons unsalted butter

2 cups sliced cremini mushrooms

3 shallots, peeled and cut into rings

1 clove garlic, peeled and minced

½ teaspoon brown sugar

2 teaspoons soy sauce

2 tablespoons balsamic vinegar

3 or 4 sprigs fresh thyme, plus extra for sprinkling

1. Preheat oven to 375°F.

2. Lay the puff pastry dough rectangles on a greased baking sheet. Sprinkle both rectangles with a generous layer of cheese, leaving a crust-like border around the outside of the pastry without any cheese.

3. In a large skillet over medium heat, add the butter. When melted, add the mushrooms, shallots, garlic, brown sugar, soy sauce, and vinegar. Stirring often, let the mushroom mixture cook and soften for 8 to 10 minutes, or until the shallots soften and begin to caramelize. Remove from heat and stir in the thyme.

4. Use a slotted spoon to add the mushroom mixture to the top of each pastry, leaving a border around the outside of each pastry uncovered.

5. After all mushroom mixture is used, sprinkle the top of each pastry with more cheese and a bit more thyme.

6. Crimp the edges of the pastries with fork

7. Bake for 20 to 25 minutes, or until the pastries are golden brown. Let rest for 5 minutes before serving.

PHYLLO CRAB BITES

Fresh crab starters are a popular menu item in our household. In addition to crab artichoke toasts or crab puffs or crab Rangoon, these phyllo crab bites will top the list. In the fall, we often head out to our West Coast shorelines when the tide is slack to catch fat, fresh Dungeness crab. These species of crab have soft white meat and the best meat yield, too. I'm sure you'll love the crunchy baked phyllo contrasted with the savory flavors of crab and the cheeses.

Makes 12 bites

1½ cups (about 12 ounces) fresh lump crab meat, finely chopped

⅓ cup finely chopped green onion, finely chopped

2 tablespoons fresh dill, finely chopped

½ cup (about 4 ounces) softened cream cheese

⅓ cup mayonnaise

¼ cup grated fresh Parmesan cheese

1 cup shredded Monterey jack cheese

Salt and fresh cracked black pepper, to taste

12 phyllo sheets

4 tablespoons melted butter

1. Spray a 12-cup mini-muffin tin with cooking spray.

2. Preheat the oven to 350°F.

3. In a mixing bowl, add the crab meat, green onion, dill, cream cheese, mayonnaise, Parmesan cheese, and Monterey jack. Mix until well combined and season with salt and pepper.

4. Take 2 phyllo sheets and lay them out (one on top of the other). Cut into four strips. Take each strip and cut into three, to make 12 squares. Each strip (consisting of the 3 squares just cut) will make one phyllo cup. Next, take the first square (two thin sheets) and lay them out. Place the second square on top, and the third on top of the second. You will need a total of 6 squares for one phyllo cup. Take the stack just created and place it into the mini-muffin tin. Some of the phyllo sheets should extend onto the sides of the pan. Repeat with the remaining phyllo sheets. Generously brush melted butter over each phyllo sheet cup.

5. Add the crab mixture into each phyllo cup. Repeat with the remaining crab mixture. Transfer to the oven and bake in the preheated oven for 20 to 25 minutes, or until the cheese is melted and the phyllo turns light golden brown. Remove from oven and serve warm or at room temperature.

PRETZEL BITES WITH CHEDDAR CHEESE SAUCE

Homemade pretzel bites are ideal while enjoying a weekend football game or FIFA soccer match. This classic American snack far outshines the bland commercially available pretzels found in malls and airports. The baking soda added to the water is an important step. Boiling the pretzel dough in the water with baking soda gives the pretzels their essential brown color and fluffy texture. They'll be a hit with your family and friends—so be sure to save some for the cook.

Makes about 5 dozen

PRETZEL BITES:

1½ cups warm water

2¼ teaspoons instant yeast

2 tablespoons melted butter

1 tablespoon brown sugar

1 teaspoon salt

3-4 cups all-purpose flour

½ cup baking soda

1 egg, beaten

½ tablespoon water

Coarse salt, as needed, for sprinkling

(Continued on next page)

1. In the bowl of a stand mixer, add the warm water and instant yeast. Whisk together and add the melted butter, brown sugar, and salt. Whisk until combined. Fit the dough hook to the mixer and turn on low speed. Slowly add in 3 to 4 cups of the flour, ½ cup at a time, until the mixture is combined and pulling away from the sides. Note: You may end up with extra flour (up to one cup) depending on the moisture of the dough.

2. Place the dough out onto a lightly floured surface. Knead by hand for 2 minutes and then shape into a ball. Place the dough ball in a large mixing bowl that has been lightly coated with cooking spray. Cover and let rest for 10 minutes. While the dough is resting, bring a large pot of water and the baking soda to a boil. Cut the dough into six equal pieces. Roll each piece into 1-inch-long ropes. Cut each rope into 1½-inch bites.

3. Preheat the oven to 425°F.

4. Line two baking sheets with parchment paper.

5. Add each piece of cut dough into the boiling water (work in batches) and let cook for 20 seconds. Remove from the water with a slotted spoon and place the pretzel bites on the

(Continued on next page)

CHEDDAR CHEESE SAUCE:

¼ cup salted butter

¼ cup all-purpose flour

2¼ cups whole milk

2 cups grated mild cheddar cheese

¼ teaspoon salt

¼ teaspoon fresh cracked black pepper

¼ teaspoon ground mustard

baking sheets evenly spaced about 1 inch apart. In a small bowl, combine the egg and water. Beat together. Brush the beaten egg wash over each pretzel bite and then sprinkle with coarse salt. Transfer the baking sheet to the oven and let bake for 12 to 15 minutes, or until golden brown.

6. In the meantime, make the Cheddar Cheese Sauce. In a medium saucepan over medium-low heat, melt the butter. Once melted, add the flour, and whisk together until no lumps remain. Increase the heat to medium and slowly whisk in the milk. Let cook over medium heat, whisking often for about 5 minutes. The mixture will thicken as it cooks. Next, add the cheese, salt, pepper, and ground mustard. Whisk to combine until smooth. Season with additional salt and pepper to taste and serve warm.

7. Serve warm with the Cheddar Cheese Sauce.

PROSCIUTTO ASPARAGUS SPIRALS

This is one of my favorite recipes when my garden yields fresh young asparagus. The mouthwatering blend of asparagus, prosciutto, and herbed cream cheese make a unique puff pastry delight. If you can't find prosciutto, thin-sliced soppressata, capicola, or pancetta will also work well. I enjoy serving these with an afternoon tea or as a healthy after-school treat.

Makes 30 spirals

6 tablespoons whipped cream cheese

1 tablespoon Pecorino Romano cheese

1 tablespoon fresh grated Parmesan cheese + more for seasoning

1 tablespoon Italian seasoning

½ teaspoon granulated garlic powder + more for seasoning

¼ teaspoon (or depending on your heat level) cayenne pepper

Salt and fresh cracked black pepper, to taste

1 package (17.3 ounces) thawed puff pastry sheets

8 slices prosciutto

30 medium asparagus spears, washed and trimmed

1. Preheat the oven to 400°F.

2. Prepare two baking sheets with parchment paper or grease the pans with olive oil.

3. In a bowl, add the cream cheese, Pecorino Romano and Parmesan cheese, Italian seasoning, garlic powder, and cayenne. Mix until well combined and season with salt and pepper.

4. Roll out the puff pastry then spread the cheese spread evenly over each dough. Cover each dough with the prosciutto (4 slices per dough). Then cut the dough-prosciutto into 30 thin strips. Using a twisting formation, wrap each prosciutto-lined dough around each asparagus stalk.

5. Sprinkle the top of each asparagus spear with black pepper, a little grated Parmesan, and garlic powder. Bake, seam-side down, for 15 minutes, or until the crust turns light golden brown. Remove from oven and serve warm or at room temperature.

PUMPKIN, SPINACH, ZUCCHINI, AND CHEDDAR MUFFINS

In addition to being delicious, these muffins hit several checklists with healthy spinach, pumpkin, zucchini, rich cheddar, and tangy feta cheeses. They'll be certain to convert a "non-muffin" eater to a believer! If you don't have fresh pumpkin, you can use canned pumpkin, but not canned pumpkin pie blend. Reduce the amount of fresh pumpkin to 2 cups of canned. They're so versatile that these muffins can be served with a brunch or even with dinner.

Makes 18 muffins

2¼ cups fresh pumpkin, cubed

3 cups chopped fresh spinach

1 small zucchini, grated

2 eggs

1 cup whole milk

1 cup crumbled feta cheese

½ cup grated cheddar or fresh Parmesan cheese

Salt and fresh cracked black pepper, to taste

2 cups all-purpose flour

4 teaspoons baking powder

1. Begin by cooking the pumpkin cubes until soft. This can be achieved by roasting under the broiler in the oven, steaming, or simply microwaving for 4 to 5 minutes until soft and cooked through.

2. In a mixing bowl, add the spinach and zucchini and cover with the cooked pumpkin cubes. Cover the bowl with plastic wrap and set aside.

3. Preheat the oven to 350°F.

4. Grease a muffin tray or line with paper liners.

5. To the bowl with the pumpkin and spinach, add the eggs, milk, and the feta and cheddar cheese. Mix until well combined then season with salt and pepper. Next, add the flour and baking powder and mix until just combined. Note: The mixture should be smooth and not lumpy. Scoop the muffin batter into the prepared muffin tin, filling to the top.

6. Transfer the muffins to the preheated oven and bake for 20 to 30 minutes, or until cooked through and a toothpick inserted into the center comes out clean. Remove the muffins and allow to cool before removing the muffins from the tins. Serve warm.

ROASTED RED PEPPER PHYLLO QUICHE BITES

When your day calls for a brunch menu, be sure to include these Roasted Red Pepper Phyllo Quiche Bites. These bites are one of my go-to recipes that in addition to being tasty are also visually appealing. There's just enough quiche in each bite that is delightfully offset by the crunch of the toasted phyllo. Include these flavorful quiche bites with the Apple, Onion, and Bacon Scones (page 44) on your brunch table.

Makes 12 bites

4 sheets phyllo pastry
dough

8 large eggs

¾ cup whole milk

¼ teaspoon salt

¼ teaspoon fresh
cracked black pepper

1 cup chopped
marinated roasted red
peppers, divided

¾ cup shredded low-
fat cheddar cheese,
divided

⅓ cup chopped green
onions

1. Preheat oven to 350°F.

2. Stack 4 phyllo pastry sheets one on top of the other. Cut the phyllo pastry (4 sheets thick) into 12 squares. Spray a 12-cup mini-muffin tin with cooking spray and arrange the phyllo squares in each muffin cup, offsetting the corners to create layers.

3. To a bowl, add the eggs, milk, salt, and pepper and whisk until combined. Distribute half of the chopped roasted red peppers and cheese evenly between each of the 12 muffin cups. Add the green onions to each muffin cup. Next, pour the egg mixture evenly into each cup and top with the remaining peppers and cheese. Bake for 18 minutes, or until the egg is set and the phyllo turns light golden brown. Remove from oven and serve warm or at room temperature.

SPANAKOPITA

Spanakopita means "spinach pie," and this traditional recipe highlights the savory richness of spinach combined with tangy feta cheese baked in a crisp, flaky phyllo pastry. When I work with phyllo dough, I make sure the thin, fragile sheets are completely thawed. And I also keep a damp towel over the sheets while working with them so they remain pliable and don't dry out. The work spent on this time-honored Greek dish is well worth the effort. I enjoy preparing and serving spanakopita on a late spring afternoon—anticipating the warmer weather to come.

Makes 18

3 teaspoons olive oil

¾ cup finely diced white onion

3 (10-ounce) packages frozen chopped spinach, thawed and squeezed dry

3 eggs

3 tablespoons dried parsley

6 teaspoons dried dill

¾ teaspoon salt

¾ teaspoon fresh cracked black pepper

1¼ cups crumbled feta cheese

16 sheets phyllo dough, thawed

¾ cup melted butter

1. Preheat the oven to 350°F.

2. Butter a 9 × 13–inch pan and set it aside.

3. In a skillet, over medium-low heat, add the olive oil. When hot, add onion and cook until slightly browned. Add the spinach and stir to combine with the onion. Remove the spinach mixture from the heat and set aside. Allow to cool to room temperature.

4. In a medium bowl, add the eggs, parsley, dill, salt, pepper, and feta cheese. Add in the spinach mixture and stir until combined. Set this aside.

5. Lay 1 phyllo sheet onto a greased baking pan. Brush melted butter on top of the sheet and up the sides. Do this for 8 phyllo sheets. Add the spinach filling on top in an even layer. Lay 1 phyllo sheet on top of the spinach mixture and brush melted butter on top of the sheet. Do this for 8 phyllo sheets. Cut (or score) it into 18 squares (or however big you want the pieces) prior to baking. Note: Phyllo is very fragile and crispy after it bakes, so this will allow you to portion it later without breakage.

6. Transfer the pan to the preheated oven and bake for 45 to 50 minutes, or until the top of the phyllo is golden brown. Remove from the oven and let it sit for 5 minutes before serving.

EVENINGS & AFTER DINNER

Who doesn't love the smells of fresh-baked treats when they come home after a long day at work, school, or trip? There's nothing like taking in the tantalizing aroma of the enticing Garlic Naan (page 133) as it cooks in a well-seasoned cast-iron skillet. My homemade Dinner Rolls (page 128) will also hit the spot with a side salad or a main dish of Cobb Salad. Evening baking doesn't have to be restrained to the indoor kitchen. Many cooks have opted to expand their culinary delights to the outdoors with a kitchen setup that often includes a brick or stone oven. These outdoor ovens are ideal for baking Pita Bread (page 134) or a crispy, authentic, thin-crust pizza from homemade Pizza Dough (page 137). After dinner, as your family and guests taste my Carrot Cake with Ultimate Cream Cheese Frosting (page 141), there'll be many mmmms, ooohs, and aaahs. If you've got chocolate lovers in-house, their needs will be satisfied with the decadent Lacey's Molten Lava Cakes (page 154) or my rich, creamy, German Chocolate Cake with Coconut Pecan Filling (page 150). These are but few of the After Dinner baking recipes in this section that will certainly pique your interest to keep you baking through the day.

CHEESY BUTTERMILK QUICKBREAD

It's just lovely when you can have a delicious bread recipe that's quick to make. My Cheesy Buttermilk Quickbread fits the bill. The characteristic tanginess of buttermilk works well with the mozzarella and Parmesan cheeses. If you don't use buttermilk often, you can use either powdered buttermilk or add 1 tablespoon of white vinegar to 1 cup whole milk. Either way, after about 15 minutes of prep time, you'll be putting this delightfully tender bread in the oven.

Makes 1 loaf

2 cups all-purpose flour

2 tablespoons sugar

1½ teaspoon baking powder

½ teaspoon baking soda

½ teaspoon salt

1 cup buttermilk

1 egg

¼ cup melted butter

1 cup grated mozzarella cheese

¼ cup grated Parmesan cheese

1. Preheat the oven to 350°F.

2. Grease a loaf pan with cooking spray and set aside.

3. In a mixing bowl, add the flour, sugar, baking powder, baking soda, and salt. Whisk together until combined.

4. In a separate bowl, add the buttermilk and egg. Whisk together until combined. Then whisk in the melted butter. Now, add the buttermilk mixture to the flour mixture and combine. Then fold in the grated cheeses.

5. Transfer the mixture to the prepared loaf pan and bake in the preheated oven for 1 hour, or until a toothpick inserted in the center of the bread comes out clean. Remove from the oven and let rest for several minutes before serving.

DINNER ROLLS

Dinner rolls have been a traditional part of many American suppers. You will delight in the simple yet robust flavor of the dinner rolls from this recipe. Whether I have prepared a dish of beef bourguignonne, chicken marsala, or a hearty Cobb salad for a main meal, these are my go-to rolls with just a hint of sweetness. If you have leftovers stored in the refrigerator, you can heat them up quickly in an air fryer or oven.

Makes 20 rolls

4½ cups all-purpose
   flour, divided
1½ tablespoons instant
   yeast
¼ cup sugar
1 teaspoon salt
1¼ cups warm milk
¼ cup softened butter
1 large egg
2 tablespoons melted
   butter

1. Add 3 cups of flour, yeast, sugar, and salt to the large bowl of a stand mixer. Stir together, then add in the warm milk, softened butter, and egg. Attach the dough hook to the stand mixer and turn to the lowest speed. Mix until the flour is incorporated, scraping down the sides of the bowl as necessary. Increase the speed to medium and beat for 2 minutes. Add ½ cup of flour and blend with the dough hook until it's fully incorporated. Add another ½ cup of flour and repeat, mixing at medium speed for another 1 to 2 minutes, or until a ball of dough is formed. Note: Add up to ½ cup of additional flour until the dough ball is slightly sticky and pulls away from the sides of the bowl.

2. Place the dough in a lightly greased bowl, cover with a towel, and let the dough rise for 30 minutes at room temperature. Remove the towel and deflate the dough by lightly punching it down. Pinch off pieces of dough to form 20 equally sized dough balls. Transfer the rolls to a lightly greased 9 × 13–inch baking dish. Cover the dish with a towel and let rise for an additional 30 minutes at room temperature.

3. Preheat the oven to 375°F.

4. Bake the rolls for 15 to 17 minutes, or until golden brown and cooked through. Note: If the rolls start browning too quickly, loosely tent with aluminum foil.

5. Brush baked rolls with the melted butter and enjoy warm or let cool and store in the refrigerator for up to one week.

GARLIC KNOTS

Homemade garlic knots never last long in our household. These fluffy and soft treats are a family favorite repeatedly asked for with every Italian meal or antipasto salad. They are super easy to prepare, and I always make sure to have extra marinara on the side for dipping.

Makes 18 knots

DOUGH:

3¾ cups all-purpose flour + additional is necessary

1½ teaspoons granulated sugar

2¼ teaspoons active dry yeast

2 teaspoons salt

1½ cups warm water + additional is necessary

2 tablespoons olive oil

GARLIC TOPPING:

½ cup butter

6 cloves garlic, peeled and minced

½ cup fresh flat leaf (Italian) parsley, minced

1½ teaspoons garlic salt

¼ cup fresh grated Parmesan cheese

1. Begin by making the dough. In the bowl of a stand mixer fitted with the dough hook, add the flour, sugar, yeast, and salt. Mix to combine. Turn the mixer on low speed and add the warm water and olive oil. Beat until the dough forms a ball around the hook. Note: If the dough is too sticky, add additional flour, 1 tablespoon at a time, until the dough comes together in a solid ball. If the dough is too dry, add additional water, 1 tablespoon at a time. Scrape the dough onto a lightly floured surface and gently knead into a smooth, firm ball.

2. Grease a large bowl with cooking spray. Add the dough, cover the bowl with plastic wrap, and place the bowl in a warm area to rise for 1 to 2 hours, or until double in size.

3. Turn the dough out onto a lightly floured surface and divide it into 2 equal pieces. Place each round of dough onto a piece of plastic wrap and let rest for 10 minutes. Dust the top of each dough with a light sprinkling of flour and, using a sharp knife, slice each into quarters. Press each quarter into a rectangle, then slice in half again. You should now have 16 pieces of dough. Dust each piece with a little flour and quickly shape into individual balls. Roll out each ball into a long rope then tie into a knot. Place the knots on the prepared baking sheet, covered loosely with plastic wrap, and let rise another 30 minutes.

(Continued on next page)

4. Preheat the oven to 450°F.

5. Remove the plastic wrap and place the garlic knots in the preheated oven. Bake for 20 minutes, or until knots are golden brown.

6. Cool for 5 minutes.

7. To make the Garlic Topping, melt the butter in the microwave until warm, then add the garlic, parsley, and garlic salt. Mix well and spread on top of the knots. Top with the grated Parmesan cheese and serve warm.

GARLIC NAAN

Traditional naan is an unleavened Indian bread and has Persian roots. When dining in almost any Indian restaurant, you will find some type, or several types, of naan on the menu. Garlic Naan is my family's preferred variety of naan. We enjoy this aromatic bread with not only our favorite Indian dishes, but also as an afternoon snack with creamy curry. Make sure the cast-iron skillet is preheated well to give the naan a nice crust.

Makes about 10 naans (depending on size formed)

DOUGH:

¼ cup warm water

2 teaspoons granulated sugar

1½ teaspoons instant yeast

¾ cup warm milk

¾ cup plain Greek yogurt

¼ cup vegetable oil + 2 tablespoons for cooking

2 cloves garlic, peeled and minced

4 cups all-purpose flour + more for dusting

1 teaspoon baking powder

1 teaspoon salt

BUTTER TOPPING:

3 tablespoons butter, melted

2 cloves garlic, peeled and minced

1 teaspoon chopped fresh cilantro

1. In a bowl, add the water, sugar, and yeast and stir to combine. Let sit for 5 to 10 minutes or until foamy. Add the milk, yogurt, ¼ cup of the oil, garlic, flour, baking powder, and salt. Mix until the dough comes together with your hands. Turn the dough out onto lightly floured surface. Use floured hands to knead the dough until smooth, 3 to 5 minutes. Lightly grease the same mixing bowl with cooking oil. Transfer the dough to the bowl and cover with plastic wrap. Let rest at room temperature for about 1 hour or until doubled in size.

2. When ready to cook, divide the dough into 10 equal pieces. Roll into balls, then use a rolling pin to roll each piece of dough into a large oval. Heat a large cast-iron skillet over medium-high heat. Grease the skillet with ½ teaspoon of the extra oil. Place one piece of the naan in the oiled hot skillet and cook until bubbles form on top, 1 to 2 minutes. While cooking, brush the top with a little oil. Flip and cook for another 1 to 2 minutes, or until large golden spots appear on the bottom. Remove from the skillet and wrap in a clean kitchen towel. Repeat with the remaining naan. Note: Keep them wrapped in a towel while you work so they stay warm until you serve.

3. For the Butter Topping: Simply combine the melted butter, garlic, and cilantro and brush over the top of the cooked naan. Serve warm.

PITA BREAD

This Middle Eastern pocket bread has become a staple in kitchens across America. Pita bread is chewy and tasty while being sturdy enough to hold sandwich fillings for a quick and easy lunch. While the dough is baking, it puffs up and separates into two layers then slowly collapses after it is removed from the oven. It is important to make sure that your pizza stone or cast-iron skillet is preheated so that the pita obtains its maximum puff.

Makes 8 pitas

1 cup warm water

1 tablespoon granulated sugar

2¼ teaspoons (1 package) active dry active yeast

3 cups all-purpose flour, divided + more for dusting

1 tablespoon extra-virgin olive oil

1¾ teaspoons salt

1. Preheat a pizza stone (or cast-iron skillet) in a 400°F oven.

2. In the bowl of a standing kitchen mixer, add the warm water, sugar, and yeast along with 1 cup of flour. Whisk everything together until uniform and set aside for 15 minutes. The mixture should bubble and foam. Add the olive oil and salt, along with 1½ cups of flour. Mix on low speed, using a dough hook attachment, until the dough is soft and no longer sticks to the sides of the bowl. If it does stick, add an additional ¼ cup of flour at a time. Knead on low for 5 to 6 minutes. Remove the dough from the bowl, turn it out onto a floured work surface, and form the dough into a ball.

3. Lightly oil a large bowl and place the dough inside. Cover the bowl with a kitchen towel. Allow the dough to rise in a warm area for 2 hours or until doubled in size.

4. Remove the dough from the bowl and place onto a floured work surface. Form the dough into a large ball and cut it into 8 pieces.

5. Form each piece of dough into a small ball, pulling dough from the sides and tucking the ends underneath the bottom. Place the balls about 1 inch apart onto the floured work surface and cover them with a lightly oiled piece of plastic wrap. Allow the dough to rest for 30 minutes.

6. Once rested, roll the dough balls out into flat and round pitas, about ¼ inch thick. Allow the dough to rest for another 30 minutes.

7. Place the pita bread dough onto the preheated pizza stone and cook until the bread begins to puff up and the bottom has browned, about 2 or 3 minutes. Care-fully turn over and cook for another 2 minutes. Wrap the cooked pita in a clean dish towel as you continue cooking the rest of the pita to keep them warm before serving.

PIZZA DOUGH

It has been argued over time that pizza was not invented by the Italians, but this beautiful country has certainly been the foundation of today's pizza. In fact, all over Italy there are myriad variations and types of pizza. My easy recipe will help you create some pizza favorites of your own. I like to use "00" or doppio zero flour for my pizza dough. This powder-fine flour has less protein than all-purpose flour. In turn, the pizza crust is flakier than the more chewy or "doughy" crust made with all-purpose flour. No need to panic, though. If all you have is all-purpose flour—this recipe will work just as well.

Makes 4 or 5 pizzas

1⅔ cups warm water

½ teaspoon active dry yeast

4 cups "00" flour

2 teaspoons fine sea salt

1. Preheat a pizza stone in a 500°F oven.

2. In a large bowl, add the warm water and yeast. Stir to combine. Slowly add the flour while stirring and add the salt. Stir to combine. Let dough rest for 10 minutes to absorb the water and stir again until smooth. Note: If the dough is too sticky, sprinkle with small amounts of flour and stir just until it is no longer sticky. Do not overmix.

3. Shape the dough into a ball and place into an oiled bowl. Cover with a kitchen towel. Let the dough rise in a warm location until doubled in size, about 1½ hours. Then punch and push the dough down to remove any air bubbles. Shape the dough into a ball again and divide into 4 to 5 pieces. Roll each piece into a ball.

4. Place the dough balls on a baking sheet and dust with flour. Cover with a damp towel and allow to rest for 1 hour to become soft and elastic. Note: To achieve the ideal texture and to develop more flavor, cover the dough balls with plastic wrap and chill overnight. Remove from refrigerator at least 1 hour before baking to bring them back to room temperature.

(Continued on next page)

5. Stretch out the dough on a floured work surface into a large circle no larger than 14 inches or it will tear. Place the dough circle onto a cornmeal-covered pizza peel or backside of a flat cookie sheet and top with your favorite toppings. Bake in the preheated oven until the crust is golden brown, about 12 to 16 minutes. Remove from the oven and let cool for several minutes before slicing and serving.

BLUEBERRY LEMON CAKE

Blueberries and lemons are a delicious combination in this cake, especially in the silky and rich buttercream frosting. Fresh blueberries yield the most authentic blueberry flavor, but store-bought blueberries work wonders, as well. I am often asked to bring this cake to community events, as it has become quite popular among our family friends. You'll find it irresistible.

Serves 10 to 12

CAKE:

1¾ cups all-purpose flour + 1 tablespoon to coat the berries

1½ teaspoons baking powder

¼ teaspoon kosher salt

1⅔ cups granulated sugar

¾ cup unsalted butter, room temperature

3 egg whites, room temperature

½ cup whole milk, room temperature

½ cup sour cream, room temperature

⅓ cup fresh lemon juice

1 tablespoon pure vanilla extract

1⅓ cups fresh blueberries

1 tablespoon fresh lemon zest

1. Preheat the oven to 350°F.

2. Butter and flour three 6-inch pans. Mix the dry ingredients (flour, baking powder, salt) including the sugar together in a large bowl. Beat the wet ingredients (butter, egg whites, milk, sour cream, lemon juice, vanilla) together in a medium bowl. In a small bowl, add blueberries and lemon zest. Coat with about 1 to 2 tablespoons of flour. Add the wet to the dry and mix until just combined. Fold in blueberry/lemon zest at the very end and mix until just combined. Divide the mixture evenly into the cake pans. Bake for about 30 minutes or until the centers are springy to the touch.

3. To make the Reduction, place ½ cup of the blueberries in the freezer. In a small saucepan over medium-low heat, combine 1 cup blueberries with the lemon juice, water, and sugar. Mash and stir for a minute then reduce to a simmer. Simmer until reduced by half then strain into a small bowl to chill.

4. To make the Lemon Buttercream, cream the butter in a standing kitchen mixer then sift in the powdered sugar in a few batches. Scrape the bowl down and mix until light and fluffy consistency. Add the lemon juice 1 tablespoon at a time until desired consistency and taste is reached. Transfer about ½ to ¾ cup to a small bowl and stir in the

(Continued on next page)

(Continued on next page)

REDUCTION:

1½ cups fresh
blueberries, divided

1 tablespoon fresh
lemon juice

1 tablespoon water

1 tablespoon granulated
sugar

LEMON BUTTERCREAM:

1½ cups unsalted butter,
room temperature

6 cups powdered sugar

3 tablespoons fresh
lemon juice

¼ teaspoon kosher salt

blueberry reduction 1 tablespoon at a time. Mix until you reach the desired flavor. Transfer the blueberry buttercream and around the same amount of lemon vanilla buttercream to piping bags. Snip off the tips of both. Add both bags to one piping bag and snip off the tip. Transfer the rest of the lemon buttercream to a piping bag.

5. To assemble, pipe the blueberry/vanilla buttercream between each layer. Add a thick layer of lemon buttercream to the edge. Pipe the plain lemon around the sides and smooth for a naked crumb coat. Scrape the sides and smooth cake for a naked look. Using your favorite decorative tip, pipe a circle of dollops about 1 inch from the edge of the cake. Add frozen blueberries to the inside of the circle and serve.

CARROT CAKE
WITH ULTIMATE CREAM CHEESE FROSTING

A homemade carrot cake is one of my favorite recipes. This lip-smacking version is simple to prepare and incredibly delightful to eat. While carrot cake is generally made during the holidays, it is such a culinary pleasure to enjoy, I recommend making it anytime. This recipe is also special because it is infused with fragrances and ingredients like thick layers of rich cream cheese, vanilla, cinnamon, moist applesauce, and shredded sweet carrots. The gourmet creamy frosting can be described as scrumptious, particularly when it includes chopped pecans (or another nut of choice). This extraordinarily moist cake is super easy to prepare, flavor packed, and aromatically enticing. The primary issue with my carrot cake and frosted cream cheese topping, though, is that one slice is almost never enough.

Serves 10 to 12

CAKE:

3 cups flour

1 tablespoon baking soda

2 teaspoons ground cinnamon

1½ teaspoons salt

1¼ cups vegetable oil

⅔ cup unsweetened applesauce

1 tablespoon pure vanilla extract

1¼ cups sugar

1¾ cups brown sugar

6 large eggs

3 cups shredded carrot

ULTIMATE CREAM CHEESE FROSTING:

16 ounces (8-ounce bricks) softened cream cheese

1 cup melted butter

1 tablespoon pure vanilla extract

¼ teaspoon salt

8 cups powdered sugar

Chopped pecans, as needed, for topping, optional

(Continued on page 143)

1. Preheat oven to 350°F.

2. Grease and flour three 9-inch cake pans.

3. In a medium bowl, add the flour, baking soda, cinnamon, and salt. Whisk until combined. In a large bowl, cream together the oil, applesauce, vanilla, sugar, and brown sugar. Mix in the eggs, one at a time, then stir in carrots. Next, combine the "dry" ingredients into the "wet" ingredients until combined. Pour the mixture into the prepared cake pans.

4. Bake for 35 minutes, or until a toothpick inserted into the center comes out clean. Turn the cakes out onto cooling racks and allow to cool completely.

5. To make the frosting, in a large bowl cream together the cream cheese and butter. Mix in the vanilla and salt. Add the powdered sugar, 1 cup at a time, mixing after each, until frosting is smooth and fluffy. Note: You may need a little less or a little more powdered sugar, depending on the consistency you like.

6. Assemble the cake by spreading the frosting on top of all three layers, then stacking the layers on top of each other. Then spread the frosting around the sides of the cake. Top with chopped pecans, if using, and serve.

CHOCOLATE CAKE

Did you ever wonder why chocolate cake is so popular? Well, part of the secret is that the cocoa helps release "feel good" endorphins. Therefore, it is a staple offering in restaurants, bakeries, supermarkets, and home kitchens. This rich and super chocolatey cake from scratch comes together in no time. The soft, lush chocolate frosting is a perfect partner for the tender chocolate cake. Since I have included sour cream in the frosting, leftovers of the cake should be refrigerated. For maximum flavor, let the cake come to room temperature before serving.

Serves 10 to 12

CAKE:

1¾ cups all-purpose flour

2 cups granulated sugar

¾ cup cocoa powder

2 teaspoons baking soda

1 teaspoon baking powder

1 teaspoon salt

1 cup buttermilk (or half-and-half)

½ cup vegetable oil

2 large eggs

1 teaspoon pure vanilla extract

1 cup hot coffee

FROSTING:

6 ounces semisweet chocolate, chopped

1 cup unsalted butter, room temperature

3 cups powdered sugar, sifted

¼ teaspoon salt

1 teaspoon pure vanilla extract

½ cup sour cream

1. Preheat the oven to 350°F.

2. Butter two 8-inch round cake pans and line the bottoms with parchment paper discs. Whisk all the dry ingredients together well in a large bowl. In a separate bowl, whisk together all the wet ingredients except the coffee. Slowly add the wet ingredients to the dry ingredients, mixing as you go. Once incorporated, add the hot coffee, and mix everything until there are no pockets of dry flour left. The batter will be very thin.

(Continued on page 146)

3. Divide the batter between the two cake pans and bake for 35 minutes until risen and a toothpick inserted into the center comes out clean. Allow the cakes to partially cool in the pans, then turn out onto a cooling rack to completely cool before frosting and serving.

4. For the frosting, melt the chocolate in a double boiler. Stir until smooth and set aside to cool slightly. Beat the room temperature butter in the bowl of a stand mixer with the paddle attachment for a couple minutes until smooth and noticeably paler in color. Slowly add the powdered sugar, salt, and vanilla, beating on a low-medium speed until everything is smooth. Whisk the sour cream into the partially cooled melted chocolate. Add the chocolate and sour cream mixture to the mixer bowl and beat on low speed until everything is smooth and combined. If the frosting seems a little too loose, refrigerate for 10 to 15 minutes to allow it to firm up a little.

FRESH STRAWBERRY CAKE

If you love strawberries, this recipe is for you. My Fresh Strawberry Cake recipe uses strawberries not only in the cake batter but also in the indulgent frosting. This is a perfect summertime recipe. As the name implies, it's very important to use fresh strawberries in this cake recipe. If you use frozen, you will get a mushy, messy cake.

Serves 10 to 12

STRAWBERRY CAKE:

3 cups quartered fresh strawberries

¾ cup sour cream

¼ cup milk

4 large eggs

1 teaspoon pure vanilla extract

2½ cups all-purpose flour

1½ cups sugar

2 teaspoons baking powder

½ teaspoon baking soda

½ teaspoon salt

¾ cup unsalted butter, room temperature

7 drops pink food color, optional

STRAWBERRY CREAM CHEESE FROSTING:

2 cups freeze dried strawberries

2 cups cream cheese, room temperature

¾ cup unsalted butter, room temperature

10 cups powdered sugar

1 teaspoon pure vanilla extract

¼ teaspoon salt

¾ cup chopped fresh strawberries

1. Begin by adding the strawberries to a food processor or blender and purée until smooth; should yield about 1½ cups of purée. Add the purée to a medium-sized saucepan and cook over medium heat. Allow the mixture to come to a slow boil, stirring consistently to keep it from burning, until it has thickened and reduced to ¾ cup, 20 to 25 minutes. To measure, pour the purée into a measuring cup. If it's more than ¾ cup, add it back to the pan and continue cooking. When the purée has thickened and reduced, pour into a large measuring cup and allow to cool to at least room temperature. Note: This step can be made the day before and refrigerated until ready to use.

2. Preheat oven to 350°F.

(Continued on page 149)

3. Prepare three 8-inch cake pans with parchment paper in the bottom and cooking spray on the sides.

4. Combine the strawberry reduction, sour cream, milk, eggs, and vanilla extract in a large bowl, then separate about 1 cup of the mixture into another bowl or measuring cup. About 1½ cups should remain in the other bowl. Set both aside.

5. In a large mixer bowl, combine the flour, sugar, baking powder, baking soda, and salt. With the mixer on the lowest speed, add the butter about 1 tablespoon at a time, allowing it to incorporate before adding the next tablespoon. As you add more butter, the mixture will start to clump together a bit and should end up resembling wet sand. Add the larger of the reserved egg mixture (about 1½ cups) to the dry ingredients/butter mixture. Stir on the lowest speed until it's incorporated, then scrape down the sides of the bowl. Increase the speed to medium high and beat until light and fluffy, about 45 seconds to 1 minute. Scrape down the sides of the bowl. Turn the speed down to low and slowly add the remaining egg mixture in a slow stream until incorporated. Scrape the sides of the bowl, then turn speed back up to medium high and mix until well combined, 10 to 15 seconds.

6. Divide the batter evenly between the three cake pans and bake 24 to 26 minutes, or until a toothpick inserted comes out with a few crumbs. Remove the cakes from the oven and allow to cool for 2 to 3 minutes, then remove to cooling rack to cool completely.

7. To make the frosting, add the freeze-dried strawberries to a food processor and grind into a powder. It should give you a little more than half a cup of strawberry powder.

8. In a large mixer bowl, beat the cream cheese and butter together until smooth. Slowly add half of the powdered sugar and the vanilla extract and mix until smooth. Slowly add remaining powdered sugar and strawberry powder and mix until smooth. Add some salt, to taste, and set aside.

9. To assemble the cake, use a serrated knife to remove the domes from the top of the cakes so they're flat. Place the first cake on a serving plate. Add about 1 cup of frosting to the top of the cake layer and spread evenly. Add about half of the chopped strawberries and press into the frosting. Add the second layer of cake, another cup of frosting and the remaining chopped strawberries. Top the cake with the remaining layer and frost the cake with the remaining frosting. Pipe a shell border around the top and bottom of the cake. Add a few strawberries on top for decoration and refrigerate until ready to serve.

GERMAN CHOCOLATE CAKE WITH COCONUT PECAN FILLING

If you need something different to make for a special occasion, my German Chocolate Cake with Coconut Pecan Filling is just the perfect recipe. Buttermilk in the batter complements the cocoa and yields a cake with a soft and light texture. A second infusion of chocolate surrounds the outside of the cake, while the inside and top are layered with a rich Coconut Pecan Filling. You'll want to serve this as a stand-alone cake for an afternoon tea or give your guests plenty of time after dinner to make room for this outrageously decadent dessert.

Serves 10 to 12

CAKE:

2 cups all-purpose flour

2 cups granulated sugar

½ cup unsweetened cocoa powder

2 teaspoons baking soda

1 teaspoon baking powder

1 teaspoon salt

2 large eggs

1 cup buttermilk

1 cup warm water

⅓ cup vegetable oil

1½ teaspoons vanilla extract

COCONUT PECAN FILLING:

½ cup salted butter

½ cup granulated sugar

1. Preheat the oven to 350°F.

2. Butter two 9-inch cake rounds and line the bottom with parchment paper.

3. In a large bowl or standing kitchen mixer, stir together the flour, sugar, cocoa, baking soda, baking powder, and salt until combined. Add the eggs, buttermilk, warm water, oil, and vanilla. Beat on a medium speed until smooth.

4. Divide the batter evenly between the two pans. Bake for 30 to 35 minutes, or until a toothpick inserted into the center comes out clean. Cool on wire racks for 15 minutes and then turn out the cakes onto the racks and allow to cool completely.

5. To make the Coconut Pecan Filling, melt the butter in a medium saucepan over medium heat. Whisk in the sugar and brown sugar until combined. Add the egg yolks, evaporated milk, and vanilla extract. Mix well. Cook over medium heat for 12 to 14 minutes or until thickened, stirring frequently. Remove from the heat and stir in the coconut flakes and pecans. Let cool completely before assembling the cake.

½ cup brown sugar

3 large egg yolks

1 (12-ounce) can evaporated milk

2 teaspoons pure vanilla extract

1½ cups unsweetened coconut flakes

1 cup chopped pecans

CHOCOLATE BUTTERCREAM:

1 cup salted softened butter

¾ cup unsweetened cocoa powder

1 teaspoon pure vanilla extract

1–3 tablespoons milk or cream

3–4 cups powdered sugar

6. To make the Chocolate Buttercream, in a large bowl, beat the butter until fluffy using a hand mixer. Add the cocoa powder and vanilla extract and beat until combined. Add 1 tablespoon of the milk or cream to thin out. Add the powdered sugar, 1 cup at a time, and beat until combined. Add up to 2 more tablespoons of milk or cream as needed to achieve a spreadable consistency. Transfer to a piping bag to frost.

7. To assemble the cake, use half of the coconut pecan filling and spread it between the two chocolate cake layers. Spread the other half on top of the cake. Frost the outside of the cake and use a piping tip to decorate the top edge.

ITALIAN LEMON POUND CAKE

This pound cake is perfect for lemon lovers. I include both lemon juice and zest in the batter. The addition of minced fresh ginger gives the lemon a lovely kick. Then I soak the warm cake with lemon glaze and top it with a luscious, lemon cream cheese frosting.

Serves 10 to 12

3 cups all-purpose flour

1 teaspoon baking powder

¼ teaspoon salt

1 cup unsalted butter, softened

2 cups sugar

3 eggs

½ cup sour cream

4 tablespoons fresh lemon juice

1 teaspoon pure vanilla extract

1 teaspoon fresh ginger, minced

2 tablespoons lemon zest

½ cup buttermilk

LEMON GLAZE:

1½ cups powdered sugar

3 tablespoons fresh lemon juice

LEMON CREAM CHEESE FROSTING:

4 ounces softened cream cheese

¼ cup lemon juice

1 tablespoon lemon zest

2 cups powdered sugar

1. Preheat the oven to 325°F.

2. In a mixing bowl, sift the flour, baking powder, and salt and set aside. In another bowl, cream the butter and sugar until light and fluffy. Beat in the eggs, one at a time. Mix in the sour cream, lemon juice, vanilla, ginger, and lemon zest. Mix half of the flour mixture into the butter mixture. Mix in the buttermilk and add the remaining flour mixture. Mix just until the flour disappears. Pour the cake batter into a Bundt pan that has been generously sprayed with baking spray.

3. Bake for 70 to 80 minutes, or until a knife inserted in the center of the cake comes out clean. Remove the cake from the oven and allow to cool for 5 minutes. Turn the cake over on a cake platter. Spread the lemon glaze over the warm cake so the glaze can soak into the cake. Let the cake cool completely and drizzle the lemon cream cheese frosting over the cake before serving.

4. Make the glaze. In a mixing bowl, add the powdered sugar. Then whisk in the lemon juice until the mixture is smooth.

5. To make the frosting, in a mixing bowl, add the cream cheese, lemon juice, lemon zest, and powdered sugar. Mix until smooth and creamy.

LACEY'S MOLTEN LAVA CAKES

Lacey is one of my closest friends. She is good at many things. For instance, she is a fantastic mother, a loving wife, an exceptional businesswoman, and an outstanding leader. With all that said, however, Lacey is not a baker. Or so I thought. Then I had a revelation about Lacey. Lo and behold, I was shocked to discover she bakes the most amazing lava cakes on the planet. I enjoy them so much I had to include Lacey's recipe in this book. No matter how many of these buttery, bittersweet chocolate jewels you eat, they'll leave you craving more.

Makes 4 cakes

½ cup unsalted butter

6 ounces bittersweet chocolate

2 eggs

2 egg yolks

¼ cup sugar

¼ teaspoon salt

2 tablespoons all-purpose flour

1. Preheat the oven to 450°F.

2. Butter and lightly flour four ramekin dishes (6-ounce size preferred). Tap out the excess flour. Set the ramekins on a baking sheet. In a double boiler over simmering water, melt the butter with the chocolate. In a medium bowl, beat the eggs with the egg yolks, sugar, and salt at high speed until thick and pale.

3. Whisk the chocolate until smooth. Quickly fold it into the egg mixture along with the flour. Spoon the batter into the prepared ramekins and bake for 12 minutes, or until the sides of the cakes are firm but the centers are soft.

4. Let the cakes cool in the ramekins for 1 minute, then cover each with an inverted dessert plate. Carefully turn each one over, let stand for 10 seconds, and then unmold. Serve immediately.

OLD-FASHIONED APPLE PIE

It is almost certain that apple pies are the most popular of all pies baked, especially by grandmas. No other pie conveys home-life quite like an old-fashioned apple pie. While there are countless variations of apple pies, this traditional Old-Fashioned Apple Pie recipe is not only foolproof to prepare, but also sure to please. It will even be well received by those who are not big apple pie fans. Each bite conveys a buttery, cinnamon-laden nutmeg flavor along with a sugary, sweet, yet tart apple filling. Your entire home will be filled with the pleasing, appetizing aromas for which apple pies are famous.

Serves 8

CRUST:

2 cups all-purpose flour

1 teaspoon salt

½ teaspoon baking powder

⅔ cup butter-flavored shortening

1 tablespoon vegetable oil

4–5 tablespoons milk

FILLING:

½–1 cup sugar, depending on apple tartness

4 tablespoons cornstarch

½ teaspoon ground nutmeg

1 teaspoon ground cinnamon

¼ teaspoon salt

5 cups thinly sliced peeled tart apples (about 4 or 5 medium-sized apples)

2 tablespoons butter

1. Begin by making the crust. In a large mixing bowl, add the flour, salt, and baking powder, and mix well. Cut in the shortening until the mixture resembles small peas. Drizzle in the oil then the milk, 1 tablespoon at a time, tossing with a fork after each addition. When the dough is thoroughly mixed, remove the dough and press firmly together with your hands as you would a snowball. Divide the dough into two balls, then roll out each piece on a lightly floured surface. Place the bottom crust into a 9-inch pie pan and set aside.

2. To make the filling, in a mixing bowl, add the sugar, cornstarch, nutmeg, cinnamon, salt, and the apples. Mix well until combined, then let stand at room temperature for at least 30 minutes.

3. Preheat the oven to 425°F.

4. Add the apple mixture to the dough-lined pan and dot with butter. Cover the pan with the top crust, seal, and flute. With a knife, slit a couple steam vents in the top crust and cover the edges with aluminum foil to prevent overbrowning.

5. Transfer the pie to the preheated oven and bake for 25 minutes. Remove the foil and bake for an additional 15 minutes. Remove the pie from the oven and let rest for 15 minutes before serving.

PEAR-ALMOND CAKE

This delicious and easy-to-make cake is a family favorite—especially when pears are in season in late summer. Although canned pears will work, if you have fresh pears, be sure to use the ones that are ripe but still are a bit firm. The aroma of toasted almonds as the cake bakes will delightfully fill your kitchen. This gorgeous cake is best served the same day it is baked.

Makes 1 cake

½ cup butter, room temperature

½ cup white sugar

2 large eggs

6 tablespoons + 1 teaspoon all-purpose flour

1¼ cups ground almonds (not almond flour)

½ teaspoon baking powder

3 ripe medium pears

⅓ cup slivered almonds

Icing sugar, as needed, for garnish

1. Preheat the oven to 375°F.

2. Grease an 8-inch springform pan and line the bottom with a round of parchment paper. Set aside. In a large bowl with an electric mixer, or in the bowl of a stand mixer fitted with the paddle attachment, beat the butter and white sugar together at medium speed until pale and fluffy. Add the eggs, one at a time, beating well after each addition and scraping down the bowl between eggs. With the mixer on low, mix in the flour, ground almonds, and baking powder. Spoon the batter into the prepared springform pan and use a spatula to even out the mixture. (Batter will be thick and fill the pan only to about an inch thick). Prepare pears, by peeling then cutting in half from the stem end to the bottom. Use a small spoon to remove the core and scrape away the thick spine that runs up to the stem end. Set aside.

3. Arrange the pear halves in a circle on the top, cut-side down and with the thin end toward the center of the cake. Sprinkle slivered almonds overtop. Bake for about 35 minutes, or until a toothpick inserted into the center of the cake comes out clean.

4. Leave the cake to cool completely in the tin, then run a knife around the outside and carefully remove the ring and base. Dust with icing/confectioners' sugar before serving.

VANILLA CAKE WITH BUTTERCREAM FROSTING

Simple—yet full of flavor. This vanilla cake boasts the ever-delicious, palate-pleasing flavors of . . . vanilla! Be sure to use pure vanilla extract to get the best flavor, aroma, and quality. Pure vanilla extract is made from the Madagascar Bourbon variety of the vanilla bean with only two ingredients: vanilla and alcohol. I like to add a small side serving of fresh berries, when in season, to each plate.

Serves 10 to 12

CAKE:

½ cup unsalted butter, softened

1 cup sugar

2 large eggs

2 cups all-purpose flour

3 teaspoons baking powder

1 teaspoon sea salt

1¼ cups buttermilk

2 teaspoons pure vanilla extract

FROSTING:

1½ cups unsalted butter, softened

6 cups powdered sugar

1 teaspoon pure vanilla extract

2 teaspoons buttermilk

1. Preheat the oven to 375°F.

2. In a mixing bowl, cream the butter and sugar. Add the eggs and gradually mix in the dry ingredients (flour, baking powder, and salt) to the wet ingredients while alternately adding the buttermilk. Mix in the vanilla.

3. Divide batter between 2 (8-inch) round cake pans that have been generously greased with butter or shortening. Bake 25 minutes, or until edges are light golden brown.

4. Allow cakes to cool in pans for 10 minutes. Transfer the cakes to cooling racks. Allow to cool completely before frosting.

5. To make the frosting, in a standing kitchen mixer fitted with the whisk attachment, whip the butter for 1 minute. Add the powdered sugar 1 cup at a time. Scrape the sides in between each addition. Mix for 30 seconds between each sugar addition. Add the vanilla and buttermilk. Mix on medium-high speed for 4 to 5 minutes. The frosting will be light and creamy. Place the mixing bowl in the refrigerator to chill for 30 minutes before frosting the cake. Whip once more before frosting.

HOLIDAYS

When I finished writing the bulk of these recipes, a thought came to me. There are several excellent recipes I prepare only during the holidays, so why not include them, too? Traditionally, one of our family favorites is left out for Santa each Christmas. My Chocolate Snowball Cookies (page 163) hit the spot, and as my children say, "Now we know why Santa stops here first—he loves your cookies, Mom." My husband has a sweet spot for Italian Almond Cookies (page 164), and we often serve them with espresso during a holiday brunch. The soft, buttery, jam-filled Linzer Cookies (page 166) are another popular favorite. They are often requested when our families come to visit for Thanksgiving—or when we go to visit them. Spring holidays (Easter, Festivus, May Day) are great times to make Overnight Cinnamon Rolls with Pecans (page 169). And who can resist traditional, chewy, almond-flavored Sugar Cookies (page 171) for any special occasion? Sugar Cookies, while made in our house during December, also go perfectly anytime, with an afternoon tea, after-dinner coffee, or a cold glass of milk. I know you'll love these recipes and perhaps they, too, will become part of your holiday baking repertoire.

CHOCOLATE SNOWBALL COOKIES

My Chocolate Snowball Cookies are a huge favorite during Christmas holiday. They are the perfect festive treat. This pastry is a combination of a rich brownie and a scrumptious cookie. Coated in powdered sugar, they are absolutely the perfect choice for all the chocolate lovers in your life. At my house, we never fail to make these cookies every year for Santa. The kids love seeing the mess from Santa's icing sugar left all over the table and floor. As a side note, my Chocolate Snowball Cookies are best served with ice cold milk—Santa's favorite.

Makes 3 dozen snowballs

1 cup unsalted butter, at room temperature

1½ cups powdered sugar, divided

¼ cup Dutch process cocoa powder

1 teaspoon pure vanilla extract

2 cups all-purpose flour

½ teaspoon salt

1. Preheat the oven to 350°F.

2. Prepare two baking sheets lined with parchment paper or a silicone sheet.

3. In a mixing bowl, add the butter, ½ cup powdered sugar, cocoa, and vanilla. Mix with an electric mixer until fluffy. Add the flour and salt and mix until the dough comes together. Let the dough cool in the refrigerator for at least 30 minutes.

4. Scoop 1 tablespoon of the dough and roll around in the remaining cup of powdered sugar then place on the prepared baking sheet. Bake for 10 to 12 minutes and then let cool on the cookie sheet for an additional 5 minutes before transferring to wire rack to cool completely.

ITALIAN ALMOND COOKIES

As Italians say about these legendary almond cookies, *"Questi bisotti sono incredibilmente deliziosi!"* (These cookies are incredibly delicious). My Italian cookie recipe is packed with ingredients that complement each other with fragrance and taste and are sweetened with a hint of nectar and vanilla extract. In Italy, they are eaten by dunking them in coffee or tea at breakfast. However, they are equally delicious by themselves any part of the day. As a tidbit of trivia, in the 1850s, Antonio Mattei created the Italian cookie, or biscuit, in Prato, a village north of Florence. The cookies were said to be well-received at international fairs in Italy, Paris, and London. I can assure you my Italian Almond Cookies will be an instant hit in your kitchen as well.

Makes 2 dozen cookies

2 egg whites

½ teaspoon fresh lemon juice

1 teaspoon fresh orange zest

1 teaspoon pure vanilla extract

1 tablespoon almond extract

2¼ cups almond flour

2¼ cups powdered sugar, divided

¼ teaspoon fine sea salt

1. In a large bowl, add the egg whites and lemon juice and whip with a stand mixer or hand mixer until stiff peaks form. Gently fold in the orange zest, vanilla, and almond extracts until combined. Set aside.

2. In another bowl, add the almond flour, 1¾ cups of powdered sugar, and sea salt. Mix together and sift into the egg whites, folding gently until combined. Note: At this point, the mixture will form a sticky dough rather than a fluffy meringue.

3. Line a baking sheet with parchment paper. Roll out the dough into 1-inch balls. Roll each ball into the remaining ½ cup powdered sugar, until well coated. Arrange on the balls on a baking sheet with some space between them for spreading and flatten slightly with the back of a spoon.

4. Leave the balls uncovered at room temperature until the tops have dried out and almost formed a "shell," about 1 hour. Note: This may take longer in humid climates.

5. Preheat the oven to 300°F.

6. When the cookies have dried, place them in the preheated oven. Bake for 20 minutes. Remove from oven and let cool before serving. The cookies can also be stored in an airtight container on the counter for up to one week.

LINZER COOKIES

The traditional, old-world confection Linzertorte was named for the Austrian city Linz. Made with a sweet almond pastry crust, the dessert is traditionally made with raspberry jam. My tasty cookie recipe for a simpler version of the torte can be made with either raspberry or strawberry jam. To make working with the cookie dough easier, it is important to keep the dough chilled. Especially appropriate for Christmas and the holidays, these Linzer cookies will brighten any dessert table.

Makes 2 dozen cookies

1 cup butter

⅔ cup granulated sugar

1 egg

1 teaspoon vanilla extract

¼ teaspoon almond extract

2 cups all-purpose flour

⅔ cup almond flour

¼ teaspoon salt

¼ teaspoon cinnamon

Powdered sugar, as needed

½ cup seedless strawberry or raspberry jam

1. In the bowl of a standing kitchen mixer, fitted with the paddle attachment, add the butter and sugar and mix. Scrape down the bottom and sides of the bowl while mixing. Add the egg, vanilla extract, and almond extract, and continue to mix until combined.

2. In a separate bowl, and the flour, almond flour, salt, and cinnamon. Whisk until combined, then add to the butter mixture. Divide into two equal parts. Shape into discs and flatten. Wrap in plastic wrap and refrigerate for 2 hours.

3. Roll the dough into ⅛-inch thickness. Cut equal number of rounds, using a cookie cutter. Transfer to a parchment paper or silicone mat–lined baking sheet. Refrigerate for 30 minutes.

4. Preheat the oven to 350°F.

5. Bake the cookies for 10 to 12 minutes, or until the edges are golden. Cool the cookies for 2 minutes on the baking sheet, then transfer to a cooling rack. Dust the top parts with powdered sugar, then add about 1 teaspoon of jam to the bottom of halves and sandwich together with the tops.

Note: Feel free to get creative with these cookies. If you like the look of traditional Linzer cookies with those fun little designs, they sell pre-made Linzer cookie cutters. Most of the sets have interchangeable shapes for the smaller "windows" inside.

OVERNIGHT CINNAMON ROLLS WITH PECANS

You will savor every morsel of these ooey-gooey sticky buns. Each bite of these beauties is packed with a plethora of extraordinary flavorings. The pastries are warm, sweet, extra soft, and the drizzled sticky topping will give you goose bumps. I assure you these rolls will perk up your lips and make your tastebuds tingle with delight. By the way, they are perfect as part of a big holiday breakfast, especially because they can be made the night before and popped in the oven the following morning. This heavenly combination of cinnamon spice and pecans can be easily substituted with your favorite nut—I often choose walnuts as my second choice. For those who might have a nut allergy, simply omit the pecans.

Makes 12 rolls

DOUGH:

1 tablespoon active dry yeast

½ cup warm water

4½ cups all-purpose flour, divided

4 large eggs

¼ cup sugar

2 teaspoon salt

¼ cup butter, softened and cut into large pieces

(Continued on next page)

1. The night before: In the bowl of a stand mixer fitted with the whisk attachment, add the warm water, and sprinkle the yeast on top. Let sit for 5 to 10 minutes or until foamy at the surface. Add in ½ cup of the flour and whisk together slowly until combined. Cover the bowl with plastic wrap and let rise for 30 minutes.

2. Remove the plastic wrap and add the rest of the flour, eggs, sugar, and the salt. Switch to the dough hook and knead on medium speed for about 5 minutes, or until smooth. Add in the softened butter and continue to knead for another 10 to 12 minutes or until smooth. You may have to hold the mixer head down when beating because it is a lot of dough to handle, depending on the size of your mixer. Once dough is completely smooth and the butter is fully incorporated throughout, cover the bowl with the plastic wrap and set out to rise for 1½ to 2 hours, or until doubled in size.

(Continued on next page)

½ cup unsalted butter, softened

½ cup white sugar

¼ cup brown sugar

1½ tablespoons cinnamon

⅓ cup finely chopped pecans

GLAZE:

4 ounces cream cheese, room temperature

3 tablespoons maple syrup

1 tablespoon milk + more if needed

3. Grease a 9 × 13–inch baking dish and set aside. Dump out the dough onto a clean and lightly floured surface and roll into a 12 × 18-inch rectangle. Spread the softened butter evenly along the surface. Sprinkle the sugars and cinnamon atop butter and then the pecan pieces. Starting with the short side (12-inch side), roll the dough up into a cylinder. Some of the filling will fall out but that is okay.

4. Cut the dough in half down the center, then those halves in half, and then repeat until you have 12 evenly sized rolls. Place the pieces, cut-side up, onto the prepared baking dish. Cover tightly with plastic wrap and place in the refrigerator to rise overnight, about 12 hours.

5. The next morning: Remove the rolls from the refrigerator and allow to rise at room temperature, about 1 to 1½ hours.

6. Preheat the oven to 350°F.

7. Bake in the preheated oven for 35 to 40 minutes, or until the rolls are golden brown on top. Start checking for doneness around 30 minutes. Let cool on the counter at least 5 minutes.

8. To make the glaze, beat the cream cheese until fluffy and smooth. Mix in the maple syrup and continue to beat until fully incorporated. Add the milk 1 tablespoon at a time, until the glaze reaches desired consistency.

9. Drizzle glaze over warm cinnamon rolls, add chopped pecans, and serve.

SUGAR COOKIES

As December rolls around each year, thoughts of baking holiday cookies begin. One of our family's all-time favorite winter cookies are sugar cookies. I like to add just a bit of almond extract to enhance the vanilla and broaden their flavor. To ensure a consistent soft and chewy cookie, make sure that all the cookies are cut thick, are uniform in size, and are spaced consistently apart on the cookie sheets. These cookies are perfectly matched with a fresh batch of homemade hot chocolate for all.

Makes 3 dozen

1 cup unsalted butter, room temperature

1 cup sugar

½ teaspoon almond extract

1 teaspoon pure vanilla extract

1 egg

2 teaspoons baking powder

½ teaspoon salt

3 cups all-purpose flour

1. Preheat oven to 350° F.

2. In the bowl of a standing kitchen mixer, add the butter and sugar and mix until smooth. Add the almond and vanilla extracts, and the egg, and mix until combined.

3. In a separate bowl, add the baking powder, salt, and flour and mix until combined. Then slowly add to the "wet" ingredients while mixing. Note: If the dough appears crumbly, keep mixing for another minute. The dough should pull away from the sides of the mixer. If the dough remains dry or stiff for your mixer, turn out the dough onto a floured surface and finish kneading the dough with wet hands.

4. Divide the dough into 3 portions and roll out onto a floured surface and cut rather thick, about ¼ inch. Arrange on a greased cookie sheet or lined with a Silpat.

5. Bake in the preheated oven for 6 to 8 minutes. Remove from the oven and let cool until firm enough to transfer to a cooling rack.

PHOTO CREDITS

INDEX

METRIC CONVERSIONS

If you're accustomed to using metric measurements, use these handy charts to convert the imperial measurements used in this book.

Weight (Dry Ingredients)

1 oz		30 g
4 oz	¼ lb	120 g
8 oz	½ lb	240 g
12 oz	¾ lb	360 g
16 oz	1 lb	480 g
32 oz	2 lb	960 g

Oven Temperatures

Fahrenheit	Celsius	Gas Mark
225°	110°	¼
250°	120°	½
275°	140°	1
300°	150°	2
325°	160°	3
350°	180°	4
375°	190°	5
400°	200°	6
425°	220°	7
450°	230°	8

Volume (Liquid Ingredients)

½ tsp.		2 ml
1 tsp.		5 ml
1 Tbsp.	½ fl oz	15 ml
2 Tbsp.	1 fl oz	30 ml
¼ cup	2 fl oz	60 ml
⅓ cup	3 fl oz	80 ml
½ cup	4 fl oz	120 ml
⅔ cup	5 fl oz	160 ml
¾ cup	6 fl oz	180 ml
1 cup	8 fl oz	240 ml
1 pt	16 fl oz	480 ml
1 qt	32 fl oz	960 ml

Length

¼ in	6 mm
½ in	13 mm
¾ in	19 mm
1 in	25 mm
6 in	15 cm
12 in	30 cm